Gardening Basics

EVERYTHING YOU NEED TO KNOW

TO GET STARTED

TIME-LIFE BOOKS, ALEXANDRIA, VIRGINIA

TIME LIFE
HOW-TO

Gardening Basics

Introduction

How often have you heard someone exclaim "I just don't have a green thumb!"? Smart gardeners know that it doesn't matter what color your thumb is—what matters is knowing what your plants need and when they need it. It's knowing what growing conditions a particular site has to offer, so you can choose plants that are naturally disposed to grow there. And it's knowing exactly how to do each job properly, so that you are able to give your plants the best possible care throughout the year.

This book is your guide to the exciting and rewarding world of gardening, from learning about your yard and preparing the soil to buying and planting the best-quality flowers and shrubs. We've presented each technique in a clear, easy-to-follow, step-by-step format to show you the way to success. Use this book as your personal gardening teacher; you'll see exactly how to assess your site, how deep to dig each planting hole, and where to make each pruning cut.

Of course, gardening is more than just following a set of steps to come up with the right results. It's a combination of art and science, pairing time-tested garden lore with solid, science-based techniques. Throughout this book, you'll find tips and tricks used by expert gardeners to help make your work easier and give you more time to enjoy the beauty of your own creation. With this treasure trove of horticultural wisdom in hand, you're well on your way to becoming a successful gardener. ❧

1. Getting Started

Deciding to establish a new garden is an exciting step in creating a beautiful landscape. You'll get the most rewarding results when you start the right way: by investigating your site, drawing a garden map, selecting appropriate plants, and gathering the right tools for the job.

The process of turning your ideas into reality starts with learning about your site conditions: the soil characteristics, the amounts of sun and shade, and the drainage. Perhaps you already know which plants you want to grow, and you need to find the spot that will best meet their needs. Or maybe you know exactly where you want the garden to be, and you'll choose plants that will thrive in growing conditions available there. Either way, taking the time to learn about the soil and light characteristics of your site with the simple tests explained in this chapter will help you make informed decisions about the garden's exact placement and plants.

Making a garden map is another important planning step. A map will give you an overview of your property, making it easy to see the space and the existing features. A map is also a great place to record the information you've learned about your property's growing conditions. When you get down to planning individual planting areas, you'll have all the information you need at a glance.

Of course, even the best-laid plans aren't much help if you don't have the necessary tools for digging and planting. In this section, you'll also find the basics of choosing the right tools for each task and caring for them properly so that they will last for many years. Once you have your tools and plans in hand, you'll be well on your way to creating your own dream garden. ❧

Making a Garden Map

Even if you are starting with one small garden, it will still be worth your while to make a simple map of your entire property. Having an overall plan will help guide your decisions about where and what to plant next. A map is also an excellent place to record garden information such as soil test results and sun and shade patterns.

Don't think you have to be an artist to make a garden map: a rough sketch is fine, as long as you can read it. Graph paper is a handy tool for creating a basic map. You can begin by measuring the outer dimensions of your property, then transfer them to paper, using a scale that will let you fit your whole map on one sheet and still allow room for details. When you sketch in your house, indicate doors and windows so that you can consider views from and of your house when you plan your gardens. To indicate trees, use an "x" to mark the trunk and a dotted line to show the outer reaches of branches, called the dripline.

When you've finished drawing existing features, redraw the map, if necessary, to clarify the outlines. Even for a small property, it can be helpful to create a separate key for features rather than labeling everything directly on the map.

When you are ready to plan a new garden, make photocopies of your base map or use tracing paper overlays so you won't have to redraw the original map. You may want to try different approaches on paper until you are satisfied with shape and size. Then, transfer your ideas to the site. Use garden hoses, or stakes and string, to mark the outline of new plantings and adjust as desired. Mark the final outline on a new map copy or overlay. If you would like to draw in plants, or try different designs within your garden outline, redraw the garden outline alone on a separate piece of graph paper at a larger scale, such as 1 square per 1 foot on the ground. ❧

Measure the outer dimensions of your property. Draw the outline of your property to scale on a large piece of graph paper.

HAVE ON HAND:

▶ Tape measure

▶ Pencil

▶ Eraser

▶ Graph paper

▶ Clipboard

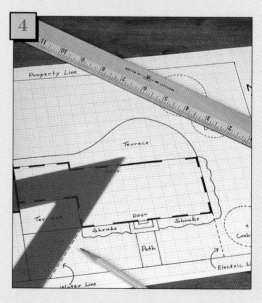

Mark the location of any rights-of-way, buried utility lines, wells, septic tanks and fields, and other underground features.

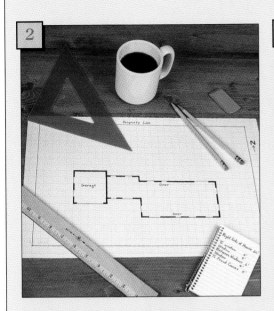

Draw in the outline of your house, marking openings for doors and windows. Also outline your garage and other outbuildings.

Sketch in other existing features, including decks, paved surfaces, trees, shrubs, hedges, fences, and garden beds.

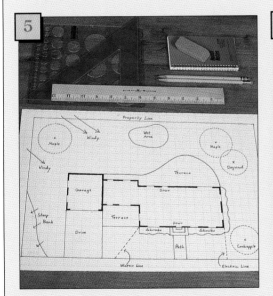

Sketch in any obvious site characteristics or problem areas, such as wet spots, steep slopes, and windy and rocky areas.

The final result is your base map. To try out new garden ideas, use photocopies or tracing paper laid over the base map.

HERE'S HOW
SETTING PLANTING PRIORITIES

Whether you're renovating an existing garden or starting from scratch, it can be tough to decide where to start. Here are some pointers to help you plan your garden priorities:

Stage 1: Work on areas you see all the time along the house and driveway. Start setting garden boundaries by planting trees, shrubs, and hedges and installing fences. Remove unwanted plantings and features. Control weeds, especially in unplanted areas. Begin a garden notebook.

Stage 2: Install any major garden projects, including decks, patios, paths, and paving. (This will avoid your damaging established plantings later on.) Gradually extend plantings away from the house. Continue to control weeds in unplanted areas.

Stage 3: Add details to existing plantings, such as edging strips to prevent lawn grass from creeping into beds. Plant vines and climbers along walls and fences. Create a continuous bed to link individual shrubs and trees, and underplant them with ground covers for easy maintenance. Add special touches, such as benches, as time and money permit.

Testing Your Soil

JAR TEST

Soil is the key to creating a healthy, beautiful garden. Its makeup can vary widely from place to place on your property, so use this simple test more than once to find out what kinds of soil you have in each garden site.

A jar test will determine your soil's texture. Texture refers to the soil's sand, silt, and clay content. Sand particles are large; clay particles are tiny. Silt particles are between sand and clay in size.

HAVE ON HAND:

► Clean 1-quart glass jar with lid

► Air-dried soil, no sticks, stones, or leaves

► Nonsudsing dishwasher detergent

► Water

► Grease pencil or masking tape

The relative amount of each in your soil affects many traits, including drainage and fertility. Soils high in sand feel gritty and are loose and easy to dig. They drain quickly and don't hold nutrients well, so need frequent watering and fertilizing. Soils high in clay are sticky when wet and hard to dig when dry. They hold more nutrients and water than sand, but they can become waterlogged. Silt particles are between sand and clay in size, have a powdery feel, and hold fair amounts of nutrients and water, letting the excess drain away.

Soil that contains approximately 40 percent silt, 40 percent sand, and 20 percent clay is known as loam. Loam provides ideal conditions for a wide range of plants. Sites high in clay or sand, however, will need amending. Both can be improved with compost or other organic matter which will loosen clay soil and will improve water and nutrient retention in sandy soil. ❧

Add 1 cup soil, 1 teaspoon detergent to jar. Fill ⅔ with water, close tightly. Shake hard for 2 minutes.

Set jar on a level surface. After 1 minute, mark the level of settled soil on the jar. This is the sand level.

After 2 hours, mark the new soil level; this is the silt layer. After 2 days, mark the final clay layer.

Compare the depth of each layer to the total depth of settled soil to determine the percentage of each.

pH TEST

Your soil's pH, or relative acidity or alkalinity, influences the nutrients available to plant roots. Know the conditions you're starting with, and you will make good decisions before planting.

Soil pH is measured on a scale of 1.0 to 14.0, with 7.0 considered neutral. A value less than 7.0 indicates acid (or "sour") soil, while a value higher than 7.0 means your soil is alkaline (or "sweet"). Most garden plants grow well when the pH is 6.0 to 7.0.

If your soil's pH is not ideal, you have two options:

HAVE ON HAND:

▶ Air-dried soil, no sticks, stones, or leaves

▶ Soil test kit

▶ Distilled water

choose plants that are naturally adapted to the existing pH, or add amendments to adjust it. You can do a simple pH test at home with a kit available at your local plant nursery, but before amending your soil, have it tested professionally, either by a private laboratory or your state Cooperative Extension Service. Most tests are inexpensive, and you'll get a detailed report on your soil's nutrient content and pH level. The results may also include specific recommendations for amendments to add for the plants you want to grow.

If you decide to plant for your conditions, azaleas and rhododendrons require acid soil, for example, while baby's breath and lilacs can tolerate alkaline conditions. If you want to grow the widest range of garden plants, add amendments such as lime (to raise pH) or sulfur (to lower pH). Compost or other organic matter can also help adjust pH to a suitable level. 🌿

Place 1 tablespoon of soil in container. Add distilled water, stir until mix is consistency of a milkshake.

Let sit for 1 to 2 hours. Add more water, if needed, to keep the mixture at the right consistency.

Lay a strip of litmus paper on mixture and let it sit for 1 minute. Remove, rinse with distilled water.

Compare the color of your test strip to the chart supplied with soil test kit to determine pH.

Determining Sun and Shade

To get the best results in your garden, take time to observe the site you're considering. A spot that looks sunny and open in April or May might be heavily shaded by deciduous trees or shrubs in midsummer. Areas that seem cool and shady in fall or spring may actually get strong sun in midsummer, as the sun changes position. If you base your garden on conditions you observe at just one time, you may select plants that aren't entirely suited to their location.

Observe sun and shade patterns in your yard over the course of one entire growing season (roughly April through September). Create a set of sun and shade maps to aid your future garden planning. They will allow you to tell at a glance how much light a particular site will receive at any time.

Most gardeners divide sun and shade into three categories: full sun, partial shade, and full shade. Full sun sites receive at least 6 hours of sunlight between 10 a.m. and 6 p.m. A partial shade (or partial sun) site gets less than 6 hours of direct sun during that time, or dappled sunlight all day. Full shade sites receive no direct sunlight.

If your site gets full sun in spring and partial shade in summer and fall, consider spring bulbs for early color and hostas, ferns, and other shade-lovers for interest later on. Where spring shade is followed by summer sun, combine early-blooming wildflowers with sun-loving annuals and perennials for a colorful, long-season display. 🌺

HAVE ON HAND:

▶ Base map

▶ Copies or overlays

▶ Pencil

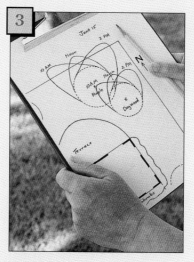

Use your property base map, indicating all permanent features. Make copies or use overlays.

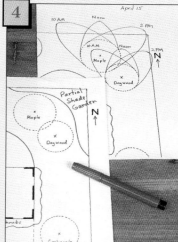

On a sunny day, observe your garden midmorning, noon, and midafternoon. Draw in shaded areas.

Repeat Step 2 every other month during growing season, drawing sun and shade patterns. Date maps.

When considering a site for a new garden, refer to maps or overlays to determine appropriate plants.

Understanding Drainage

Checking soil drainage is a critical step in learning about a prospective planting site. Drainage refers to the movement of water over the soil surface, below the surface, and between individual soil particles.

Surface drainage depends largely on the steepness of ground slope. On a gentle slope, water may soak in and excess run off. On a steep slope (especially if the soil is clay), water may run off before it can be absorbed. Flat sites absorb all the water they can, but excess will puddle on top until water already in the soil drains away. In most cases, gently sloping or flat spots will be fine for a garden.

Drainage below the surface depends on conditions below the topsoil layer. If the upper 8 inches of soil feels loose and crumbly, but water collects on the surface after heavy rains, there may be a compacted layer (called hardpan) below the topsoil. Hardpan keeps water in topsoil from draining through the subsoil. Or you may have water coming up from an underground spring. Subsurface drainage problems are usually hard to fix. You might either choose plants that thrive in wet conditions or build raised beds to provide better drainage.

The third aspect of drainage is the way water moves between soil particles. Sand particles stay loose, allowing water to drain quickly. In sandy soil, water may drain through faster than roots can absorb it. Clay particles can pack together tightly and become waterlogged, drowning plant roots. Loamy soils hold enough water while letting excess drain away. 🌸

HAVE ON HAND:

▶ Trowel

▶ Water

SIMPLE TEST. *Dig a hole about 1 foot deep and 6 inches wide. Fill the hole with water; let it drain.*

Add water to refill hole. If it takes more than 8 hours for the water to soak in, your soil is poorly drained.

SPOTTING PROBLEMS. *If you strike a dense layer before digging 2 feet deep, you have hardpan.*

If soil does not drain, use plants that will thrive in wet soil, or build one or more raised beds.

Working with Garden Tools

CHOOSING TOOLS

When you shop for garden tools, don't be overwhelmed by the wide array of equipment available. You only need a few basic tools to get started. A spade and spading fork for digging, a metal garden rake for smoothing, and a trowel for close work around plants are musts. Other basics include pruning shears for trimming and a shovel for moving soil and mulch.

Buying good-quality tools will save the cost and hassle of buying replacements later. Bargains tend to break quickly, make your job harder and litter your storage area with unusable tools.

Check all parts of digging tools: the blade, the handle, and the connection between the two. A high-carbon or stainless steel blade will last longer than regular steel. Forged blades, made from thick metal, are stronger and more durable than stamped blades, which are cut from a metal sheet and have a fold where joined to the handle.

High-quality tools usually have wooden or plastic-coated steel handles. Ash and hickory are the most durable and desirable woods for handles. Avoid buying tools with painted handles; the paint may cover knots or flaws in the wood. Long, straight handles provide more leverage for digging, while shorter, "D"-grip handles offer more control and prying power. Choose the length that feels most comfortable for your height.

Look for tools with "solid-socket" or "solid-strap" construction. Both have metal extending from the blade to cover part of the handle. One-piece construction makes them very strong. Cheaper "tang-and-ferrule" construction is made with a thin metal extension from the blade-top into the handle. A metal collar surrounds the base of the handle, secured by a rivet or bolt. This type of construction is less expensive but also less durable than either solid-socket or solid-strap.

A footrest makes it easier to push a blade into soil and protects your leg if your foot slips off the blade.

Solid-socket/solid-strap construction means a sturdy, durable connection between blade and handle.

Check wooden handles. The "grain" should run straight down the handle, with no knots or cracks.

If your soil is rocky or hard to dig, choose a spading fork with thick tines; thin ones will quickly bend.

CLEANING TOOLS

After a day in the garden, you may be tempted to toss your tools into the garage and head inside for a cool drink. But it's worth taking a few minutes to clean your tools after each use to keep them in top shape. With regular maintenance, they will repay your investment with many years of service.

At the end of each gardening session, remove damp soil on blades so rust won't develop. Never use a metal tool to scrape soil from another tool; you'll damage both. A stiff utility brush should do the job. Or keep a bucket of sand near your tool storage, so you can plunge the blades into the sand to clean off the soil. Once metal parts are clean, coat them with a thin layer of light machine or mineral oil or spray with a lubricant to prevent rust from developing.

Handle care is important for your own comfort. A clean, smooth handle is much more pleasant to hold and is less likely to cause blisters. When necessary, sand handles lightly to smooth out rough spots. A coat of varnish, tung oil, or other sealer will help protect the wood. Replace damaged handles as soon as possible.

Brush wood scraps and clean dried sap from pruning tools (use steel wool, if needed). Oil all metal parts lightly. Check and tighten the blades as needed.

HAVE ON HAND:

▶ Wooden scraper

▶ Water

▶ Dry cloth

▶ Wire brush

▶ Motor oil on rag

▶ Sandpaper

▶ Sealer

Scrape off soil clinging to blades or tines of digging tools with a wooden or plastic scraper.

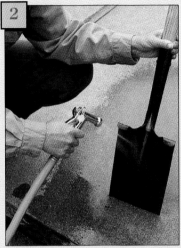

If you can't remove all the soil with the scraper, rinse it off with water, then dry the tool thoroughly.

Use a wire brush to remove rust on any metal parts, then wipe metal with an oily rag to prevent rust.

Wipe handles with a dry cloth to clean off clinging soil. Sand and seal handles to keep them smooth.

KEEPING TOOLS SHARP

A clean, sharp tool can make almost any garden job a pleasure. Sharpening your tools often will keep them in top shape, so they're always ready when you need them. A sharp blade can also be safer for you and your plants, since it will cut easily and cleanly through plants or soil; dull blades tend to slip and crush or tear stems.

The goal of any sharpening job is to create an edge that is both sharp and durable. You'll want to keep the existing angle of the cutting edge (known as the bevel), but remove nicks and improve the keenness of the edge. Before sharpening, check the existing bevel of the blade. Most spades, shovels, and hoes have a single bevel, with one flat side and one angled side. Always sharpen single-bevel tools on the angled side only; otherwise, you will create a weak cutting edge that is susceptible to damage.

A mill bastard file is the sharpening tool of choice for most home gardeners. Holding the file at a shallow angle to the blade will create the thin, sharp edge desirable for cutting and weeding tools. A steeper angle will produce a longer-lasting edge more suitable for digging tools.

File until you feel a slight buildup of metal, called a "burr," on the back side of the blade. When the burr extends all along the blade edge, turn the blade over and rub the file flat across the blade to remove the burr. 🌾

HAVE ON HAND:

▶ Protective gloves

▶ Flat file for flat-bladed tools

▶ Curved file for curved-bladed tools

▶ Oily rag

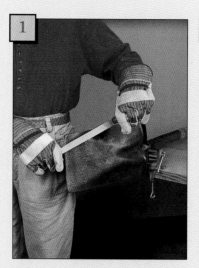

Wear gloves. Secure spade, inside of blade facing you. Hold file to match bevel angle, toward blade edge.

Push file away from blade, while sweeping it from one side of blade to the other. Use the length of file.

Give nicks a few extra strokes with the file to smooth them out, for an even, uniform edge.

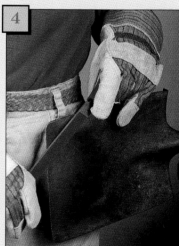

Turn blade over. Hold file flat against blade, draw back and forth to remove "burr." Wipe with oily rag.

STORING TOOLS

When you are ready to dig, plant, or prune, you want to gather your tools and start. Preparing a proper storage area for your tool collection will help ensure that your tools are ready for use and easy to find.

You don't need much room to store a basic tool collection; a corner of your garage will be fine. As your collection expands, you may want to construct a separate storage shed or toolhouse. Wherever you choose, the site should be dry to prevent metal tools from rusting, and also well lighted so that it's easy to see what you are looking for.

A well-planned storage area has racks or hanging spaces for tools and shelves or cupboards for supplies. For long-handled tools, you can make a simple rack by nailing a 2 x 4-inch strip to the wall, about 4 feet above the ground, and attaching several broom holders (available in most hardware stores). A pegboard is handy for hanging small tools. If desired, you can outline the shape of each tool in paint on the pegboard. You'll be able to see at a glance where each tool belongs and if any are missing. Choose a storage system that is comfortable and convenient for you—don't be tempted to dump your tools in a corner and deal with them later.

Don't forget to bring in other garden equipment for the winter. Drain hoses, then coil loosely and hang indoors. Wash and dry garden stakes and store them inside. 🌺

HAVE ON HAND:

▶ Motor oil on rag

▶ Fine-grit sandpaper

▶ Varnish or tung oil

▶ Files

▶ Steel wool or wire brush

Sharpen tools before putting them away in fall, so they'll be ready to use when you need them in spring.

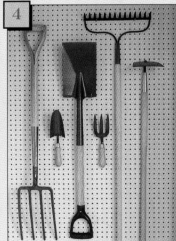

Scrape or wash off soil from metal parts; dry thoroughly. Wipe metal parts with oily rag to prevent rust.

Wipe off handles. Sand rough spots; seal with varnish or tung oil. Replace damaged handles.

Hang tools in a dry place. Remove rust spots that develop with steel wool or a wire brush, and oil again.

A Guide to Garden Tools

DIGGING

Preparing soil for planting calls for heavy-duty tools. Use hand tools for digging smaller planting holes. Tools vary widely; test weight and balance before you buy.

SPADE
Flat or slightly curved, rectangular blade. Use for lifting sod, digging beds or holes, and cutting edges along beds and borders.

ROUND-POINT SHOVEL
Curved steel blade with gentle point. Many uses: digging, moving mulch and other loose materials, and lifting plants.

CUTTING

Regular trimming will keep flowers and shrubs looking their best. Sharpen all cutting tools regularly. The work will go faster and the spread of plant disease minimized.

PRUNING SHEARS
One-hand tool with one or two cutting blades. Choose by-pass type, with two slightly curved blades. Use for stems up to ¾ inch thick.

LOPPING SHEARS
Two-hand tool with one or two cutting blades. Long handles give more leverage for cutting stems between ¾ and 1½ inches thick.

MAINTENANCE

Use these additional tools to help keep your garden looking its best. Maintenance includes weeding, moving mulch and other materials, and general garden cleanup.

HOE
Rectangular or angled metal blade on a long handle. Use for leveling soil before planting and for cultivating after planting.

METAL RAKE
Long, straight row of metal teeth. Best for leveling beds and for removing surface stones and debris to smooth soil before sowing seed.

Tools for Special Uses

Walk into any garden center and you'll be amazed by the wide variety of garden tools available. A collection of the tools shown above will help you do almost any garden job, but there are a few specialty items that can be convenient for particular tasks. 🌿

For planting large numbers of bulbs, a bulb planter can be handy. Hand-held types are best for work in prepared soil. Long-handled types can be used while standing. For heavy-duty digging, buy an auger attachment for a power drill.

SPADING FORK
Large steel fork with four, usually square or rectangular, tines. Excellent for loosening soil and lifting bulbs and perennials.

TROWEL
Small, scooped metal or plastic blade. Handy for digging small holes, lifting small plants, planting bulbs, and weeding.

HAND FORK
Three or four straight, short, metal or plastic tines. Use for loosening soil for planting, lifting bulbs and small plants, and weeding.

PRUNING SAW
Serrated, usually curved cutting blade on fixed or folding handle. Sturdy tool for cutting branches between 1½ and 3 inches in diameter.

GRASS SHEARS
Long, scissor-type blades. Use these for trimming grass and weeds along edges and around trees and shrubs, and for shearing annuals.

GARDEN SCISSORS
Resemble kitchen scissors, often with large looped handles and blunt ends. Handy for cutting flowers, deadheading, and very light trimming.

LEAF RAKE
Long, flat, wooden, bamboo, metal, or plastic tines with curved tips. Handy for cleaning up garden trimmings and fallen leaves.

WHEELBARROW
One or two wheels supporting a scooped body. Indispensable for moving mulch, compost, soil, and trimmings around in the yard and garden.

GLOVES
Cloth, leather, plastic, or rubber gloves designed for outdoor use. Long-cuffed styles provide extra protection for pruning roses and other thorny plants.

2

Hand-held sprayers have a metal or plastic tank attached to a pump. They are useful for applying liquid fertilizers, such as fish emulsion, directly to plant leaves for a mid-season nutrient boost. Use them for spraying insecticidal soap and other pest controls.

3

A 5-gallon bucket is an invaluable garden tool for hauling mulch into beds and borders and carrying debris to the compost pile. Tarps are useful for garden cleanup and leaf raking; simply gather the corners and carry or drag to your compost pile.

2. Preparing Your Planting Bed

Few gardeners are blessed with perfect soil: soil that is naturally fertile and neither too acid nor too alkaline, with a loose, crumbly texture that drains well but holds just enough moisture for good root growth. Fortunately, it's possible to improve just about any kind of soil. Each time you dig a new garden or cultivate an existing bed before replanting, you have the opportunity to build better soil in your garden.

Digging at the right time, and to the best depth for your plants, is a key step in preparing a good planting site. By loosening the soil, you'll create a layer that's easy for roots to grow through in their search for water and nutrients. A sturdy, spreading root system will support strong, healthy growth and generous flowering above ground. Careful digging will also give you the chance to get rid of weed roots, dramatically reducing your weeding chores after planting.

If your soil is less than perfect, don't despair— there are plenty of tricks you can use to get it in prime condition. You might choose to add compost, chopped leaves, or other organic matter to improve texture; amendments to change the soil pH (acidity or alkalinity), or fertilizers to supply a balance of needed nutrients. If your soil is wet or rocky, you may want to build up the soil, instead of digging down, to create a rooting layer that's deep enough for good plant growth. In this section, you'll find many suggestions for improving your planting site so that you can create a garden that will perform well for many years. 🌺

Cultivating Your Soil

SIMPLE DIGGING

When you are creating a garden for annuals, a simple dig will cultivate enough surface soil to provide good growing conditions for these shallow-rooted plants. If your soil is on the sandy side and fertile, a simple dig will be sufficient for perennial, rose, and shrub plantings.

You can dig your soil any time of the year that it isn't frozen or too wet. To test soil moisture, use a trowel to dig up a handful of soil. Squeeze the soil, then open your hand. If the soil crumbles right away, or when you tap the ball lightly, it is fine to dig. If the soil stays in a ball, wait a few days and test again. If the weather has been dry for several weeks, water the area thoroughly a few days before planting to soften the soil and make digging easier.

Before you dig your garden, remove any vegetation growing there. Simply digging or tilling grass and weeds into the soil will not get rid of them; the plants will quickly resprout. Slice just under the soil surface with a spade to sever plants from their roots. The roots will break down easily, adding organic matter to the soil. Some weeds, such as dandelions, will resprout right from the roots, so remove them as far down as possible. Pick out and dispose of strong-looking, white roots creeping horizontally through the soil. Don't compost them; they may resprout and spread through your compost pile. 🌿

HAVE ON HAND:

▶ Stakes

▶ String

▶ Spade

▶ Shovel or spading fork

▶ Rake

Mark area with stakes and string. Use spade to slice off top 2 to 3 inches of turf to remove weeds.

Start at a corner of bed; insert full shovel blade into the soil. Pull the handle toward you to loosen soil.

Twist shovel to turn soil over. Repeat steps, working backward to loosen the soil in the entire bed.

Use metal rake to smooth surface. Remove rocks and other debris before planting.

DOUBLE DIGGING

Double digging helps you provide the best possible growing conditions for deep-rooted plants such as perennials, roses, and shrubs. This technique loosens the top 18 to 24 inches of soil. Deep digging takes extra time and energy, but it helps plants thrive by providing an extra-deep zone of loosened soil. Plant roots can spread easily to search out water and nutrients. By double digging, you work organic matter deeper into the root zone to improve soil structure and fertility. This also improves drainage by breaking up the compacted subsurface layers.

Before starting a double dig, follow the same preparations as for a simple dig: squeeze a handful of soil to make sure it isn't too wet (it should crumble when you open your hand), then remove existing grass and weeds. Pick out thick, white roots as you dig; it's okay to leave fine, branching grass roots.

To avoid stepping on and compacting the loosened soil, walk on broad boards laid over the area to distribute your weight evenly. Remove the boards when you are finished. Or lay broad, flat steppingstones and then plant around them. Later on, you will be able to reach plants for maintenance without stepping directly on the soil.

After digging, your soil surface will be several inches higher than it was before. Let the soil settle for a week before planting. ❀

HAVE ON HAND:

▶ Stakes

▶ String

▶ Spade

▶ Tarp or wheelbarrow

▶ Shovel or spading fork

▶ Compost

Mark outline of bed with stakes and string. Use spade to slice just below surface to remove growth.

Working along back edge, dig trench 1 foot wide and at least as deep. Pile soil on tarp or wheelbarrow.

Loosen soil in bottom of trench; add 2 inches of compost. Dig another trench next to the first one.

Fill first trench with soil from new one. Repeat until entire bed is dug. Fill last trench with reserved soil.

Improving Your Soil

If you have less than ideal soil, you can condition it before planting. The steps you need to take depend on the special characteristics of the site (see Testing Your Soil, page 10, and Understanding Drainage, page 13), but even loam will benefit from the addition of compost.

For soil that is particularly sandy or clayey, work in organic matter, such as compost (see Here's How), to improve its structure and drainage. Where soil pH is lower than 6.2, add lime (sold as garden lime or ground limestone) to raise the pH to around 6.5 to 7.0, which is ideal for a wide range of garden plants. Elemental sulfur (sold as garden sulfur) will lower soil pH; use it on soil with a pH higher than 7.0.

If most plants in your garden grow well without regular fertilizing, your soil probably has an adequate balance of nutrients. But if your plants grow poorly without supplemental fertilizer, test your soil to check the nutrient content. Check your local garden center for kits, or ask them to recommend a soil testing laboratory. Review the test results and add fertilizers as needed to prepare a new bed.

Correct drainage problems before planting, unless you intend to grow only moisture-loving plants. First, identify the cause of the problem. If the surface soil is fairly loose but you hit a dense, compacted subsurface layer when you dig, called hardpan, deep cultivation will break it up (see Double Digging, page 23). For soil too hard or rocky to dig deeply, build a raised bed, which will add 8 to 10 inches of soil on top of the ground to give plants rooting room. To hold the soil in place, frame the bed with landscape timbers or rocks. Raised beds are useful for wet sites, since the plants will be growing in a layer of well-drained soil, rather than in the water-logged earth. 🌺

SOIL pH. *Test with kit. Add lime or sulfur as indicated in the test results; dig into the top 1 foot of soil.*

HAVE ON HAND:

▶ Soil test kit

▶ Compost or other organic matter

▶ Lime

▶ Sulfur

▶ Organic fertilizers

▶ Spade, shovel, or spading fork

▶ Rocks or landscape timbers

SOIL HIGH IN CLAY OR SAND. *Dig or till a 1- to 2-inch layer of compost or other organic matter into the top 8 inches of soil.*

Raise the pH of acid soil by 0.5 by digging in 4 pounds of lime per 100 square feet. Test again every 3 to 4 years.

Lower the pH of alkaline soil by 0.5 by digging in ½ pound of sulfur per 100 square feet. Test again every 2 to 3 years.

COMPACTED SOIL. *Improve drainage by digging deeply to loosen top 12 to 18 inches of soil. Avoid stepping on loosened soil.*

WET OR ROCKY SOIL. *Build raised beds. Use rocks or timbers as framing. Make sides 10 to 12 inches high. Fill with well-drained soil.*

HERE'S HOW

MAKE YOUR OWN COMPOST

Make your own soil amendment by composting garden trimmings and kitchen scraps. Choose a garden spot that's out of the way. You can have a freestanding pile or enclose it in a homemade or commercial bin. You'll need enough room for a pile at least 3 feet long, wide, and tall, the size necessary to generate sufficient heat.

To build the pile, layer roughly equal amounts of high-carbon and high-nitrogen materials. High-carbon materials tend to be brownish and dry; they include fallen leaves and straw. High-nitrogen materials tend to be greenish and wet; think of fresh grass clippings and vegetable peelings.

As the materials accumulate, water the pile occasionally to keep it moist but not wet. When the pile is about 3 cubic feet in size, use a pitchfork to stir up the materials. Turn the pile once or twice a week after that. The compost will be ready to use in 2 to 4 months, when it is dark and crumbly and the original materials are mostly unrecognizable.

A Guide to Soil Improvement

AMENDMENTS

Amendments help build and maintain good soil conditions. Compost and manure promote good soil structure. Lime, sulfur, and gypsum balance nutrient availability.

COMPOST
Decayed plant material. Adds nutrients and organic matter; loosens soil; improves moisture retention. Dig or till in a 2- to 3-inch layer.

MANURE
Adds nutrients and organic matter. Compost fresh manures before using them, or work them into the soil in fall before spring planting. (Caution: only cow and horse manures should be added to the compost pile.)

FERTILIZERS

Fertilizers provide significant amounts of nitrogen, phosphorus, and/or potassium, the three major plant nutrients. Most natural fertilizers are high in one or two of these.

BLOOD MEAL
Dried blood. High in nitrogen. Use sparingly: about 1 pound per 100 square feet; keep it a few inches from plant stems.

FISH EMULSION
Made with ground fish parts. High in nitrogen; also provides phosphorus and potassium. Use about 1 pound per 100 square feet. Fishy odor, may attract cats.

MULCHES

Organic mulches keep soil moist and moderate in temperature, encouraging root growth. They also release a small amount of nutrients. Replenish as needed.

SHREDDED LEAVES
Attractive and lightweight. Chop with a mower or shredder. Use a layer 3 to 4 inches deep, alone or over 1 inch of compost.

GRASS CLIPPINGS
Apply 1 inch of fresh clippings or 2 inches of dried clippings. Top with a thin layer of a more attractive mulch.

Making Leaf Mold

Leaf mold is an excellent substitute for compost, either dug into the soil or spread on the surface as a nutrient-rich mulch. It is often rather lumpy so, if you use it for mulch, fluff it with a pitchfork first to break up the clumps. Or cover it with a thin layer of shredded bark or another attractive, uniform mulch. 🌿

In fall, rake leaves into piles on your lawn or paved driveway. If you don't have many leaves from your own trees, rake and collect your neighbors' leaves. Some communities also make collected leaves available to local residents.

LIME
Ground limestone. Reduces soil acidity; adds calcium. Test soil before liming to make sure your garden needs it.

SULFUR
Mineral. Increases soil acidity. Test soil before adding to make sure you need it, and to find out how much to use.

GYPSUM
Mineral. Lowers pH, supplies both calcium and sulfur; it can also help to loosen clayey soil. Apply approximately 2 pounds per 100 square feet.

BONE MEAL
Dried, ground bones. Supplies phosphorus and calcium. Add 2 pounds per 100 square feet; dig or rake into soil to get it near roots. May be attractive to dogs.

ROCK PHOSPHATE
Mineral. High in phosphorus and calcium. Every 3 to 5 years, apply 2 to 3 pounds per 100 square feet; dig or rake into soil.

KELP MEAL
Dried, ground seaweed (shown in closeup). High in potassium; also adds other nutrients. Apply 1 pound per 100 square feet of garden.

SHREDDED BARK
Uniform and natural-looking. Use it alone in a 3- to 4-inch layer, or apply it over grass clippings or compost.

WOOD CHIPS
Attractive and relatively long-lasting. Apply a 2-inch layer over 1 inch of compost or grass clippings. Comes in a number of different sizes.

PINE NEEDLES
Good-looking and light-weight. Ideal for plants that love acid soil, azaleas, for example. Apply a layer 2 to 4 inches thick.

2 Run a lawn mower over the piles to chop the leaves into small pieces. A power mower with a bag attachment makes the job especially easy. Rake up and pile the shredded leaves. Cover them or build a wire bin to contain them and protect from wind.

3 Keep the leaves moist and fluff the pile every month with a pitchfork to encourage faster decomposition. The leaf mold should be ready by mid-spring of the following year. Finished leaf mold is dark, soft, and crumbly, with a sweet, earthy smell.

3. Planting And Transplanting

You've developed a wonderful garden plan and prepared the perfect planting site. Now it's time to get your garden growing. First you need the plants—either grown from seed, bought from a nursery or garden center, ordered by mail, or ready to be transplanted from other parts of your yard. Then you need to know the proper planting techniques to get your plants off to a healthy and vigorous start.

Plant shopping for a new garden is fun, but it's important to take a plant list with you—and stick to it. (Otherwise, consider creating a special "trial" bed, where you can grow your unplanned acquisitions until you find a good spot for them in the garden.) And, it is essential for you to inspect all new plants for pests and diseases before you buy them. Don't pay for the privilege of bringing problems home to your healthy garden.

Of course, you have the option of raising your own plants. Most annuals are easy to grow from seed, even for beginning gardeners. Perennials don't take much more skill, but they do demand more patience, since they can take two years or more to reach flowering size. When you are starting out, it's easier to purchase plants for your first garden, then experiment with seed sowing for future plantings.

In this section, you'll learn the basics of starting, growing, and buying top-quality plants and getting them settled into your garden. You'll also find guides that highlight plants for special purposes. With all of this at your fingertips, you're virtually guaranteed a great garden!

Starting Seed Indoors

With a few basic materials and a bit of patience, you can grow dozens of new plants for the price of a single seed packet.

Your planting containers should be at least 2 inches deep, with holes in the bottom for drainage. Fill your pots with moistened commercial seed-starting mix. Avoid using garden soil; it will pack down in the pots, discouraging healthy root growth, and may contain weed seeds or

HAVE ON HAND:

- ▶ 4-inch pot
- ▶ Commercial seed-starting mix
- ▶ Seeds
- ▶ Shallow pan
- ▶ Water
- ▶ Plastic bag

diseases that can harm new seedlings. After sowing seeds, place a plastic bag around the pots, using pencils or other supports to make a tent, and place under fluorescent lights or in bright but indirect sunlight (direct sun will overheat, or even cook, seedlings). When seedlings are ½ to 1 inch tall, remove the bag. Fertilize seedlings with fish emulsion or other liquid organic fertilizer.

When seedlings have two or three pairs of "true" leaves (not the first leaves on the plant, which form inside the seed), transplant to individual pots. Carefully slide seedlings out of container. Separate seedlings by holding leaves with the fingers of one hand while gently loosening roots with a pencil. Transplant to a 3-inch pot filled with moistened potting soil. With a pencil, make a hole for the roots and set them in. Gently firm the soil around roots with your fingers. Water and set in a bright place until the plants are ready for the garden. 🌿

Fill 4-inch pot with moistened soil mix to within ½ inch of the rim. Smooth surface with your finger.

Scatter small- and medium-sized seeds evenly over surface. Place large seeds about ½ inch apart.

Cover seeds with more mix, according to seed packet instructions. Lightly firm the surface.

Set in pan with 1 inch of water for 1 hour. Drain. Set pot in plastic bag. Place in warm, bright spot.

Hardening Off

Seedlings grown indoors lead a pampered life, with regular watering, even temperatures, and protection from wind. In the garden, though, they will need to adapt to less than perfect growing conditions. You can ease this transition from indoors to out through a process called "hardening off."

Hardening off means exposing seedlings to gradually longer periods of outdoor conditions, until they are tough enough to withstand wind and weather without damage. It's a critical step for getting home-grown seedlings off to a good start in the garden. It's also useful if you've purchased transplants from a greenhouse or garden center in early to mid-spring, when the plants may have been kept indoors to protect them from cold.

To decide when to start hardening off, calculate the proper transplanting time for your plants. The seed packet may give you some guidance, such as "plant after danger of frost has passed." If you buy transplants, ask the supplier when you can set them in the garden. If you are unsure of the last frost date in your area, check with a local garden center.

Mark the transplanting date on a calendar, then count back 1 to 2 weeks for the date to begin hardening off. If you aren't home during the day, set seedlings out in the early evening; bring them indoors at night. Over weekends, leave them out for a half day each day, then for a full day on Monday. Water them thoroughly in the morning, so they won't dry out before you return home.

A porch or patio sheltered from strong sun and wind is a great place to harden off seedlings. Other possible spots include under shrubs and trees, or on the north side of your house. ❧

About 2 weeks before transplanting, allow the top 1/4 to 1/2 inch of soil to dry out between waterings.

A week before transplanting, set seedlings out for 1 hour the first day in partly shady, sheltered spot.

Over the next few days, leave the seedlings out for longer periods, an extra hour or two each time.

Water often to keep plants from drying out. After a whole day out, they are ready to transplant.

Starting Seed Outdoors

Some annuals are so easy to grow that you can sow their seeds directly into the garden. You can also raise many perennials and bulbs from outdoor-sown seeds, although they tend to grow more slowly than annuals. You should sow these bulbs and perennials in a special "nursery bed," an out-of-the-way spot where the seedlings can grow and develop. After a year or two, they will be big enough to transplant to a permanent spot in the garden.

To prepare your site for planting, first loosen the soil with a simple or double digging (see Cultivating Your Soil, page 22). Lay broad boards to avoid stepping on the bed after digging; otherwise, you will compact the soil and make it harder for the roots of your seedlings to spread.

The best time to sow depends on where you live and the seeds you're planting. Check the seed packet or catalog for recommended planting times. You'll often see a reference to the "last frost date" in the recommendations. This refers to the average date of the last spring frost for your area. If you don't know your last frost date, check with a local garden center.

Once seedlings emerge, you may have to thin them out to prevent crowding. Snip less sturdy seedlings at ground level with garden scissors, as pulling them out may injure the roots of the remaining ones. Clip as many seedlings as necessary to leave the rest at the spacing recommended in the seed packet instructions.

HAVE ON HAND:

▶ Garden rake

▶ Seeds

▶ Water

▶ Scissors

Rake the prepared soil just before planting to smooth the surface. Remove any roots and debris.

Scatter small- and medium-sized seeds thinly and evenly. Rake lightly to scratch the seeds into the soil.

Place large seeds individually, at the depth and spacing indicated on the seed packet. Cover with soil.

Lightly firm the soil with palm of hand. Water gently with fine mist; keep moist until seedlings appear.

Protecting Seedlings from Frost

The one thing you can predict about the spring weather is that it will be unpredictable. One day will be sunny and summer-like; the next may bring the return of winter-like cold. Hardening off your seedlings helps them tolerate these extreme temperature changes. But if a sudden cold snap brings nighttime frost, even hardened-off seedlings will need extra protection.

Once you've set out transplants, pay close attention to daily weather forecasts to see if frost is predicted so you can take measures to protect your seedlings.

Fortunately, frost protection doesn't require fancy or expensive materials. You can use a variety of items found around the house, including plastic milk jugs (either quart or gallon), cardboard boxes, and newspapers. Or you can buy floating row covers—lightweight, polyester material available at garden centers or through mail-order garden suppliers. All of these protectors cover the plants and hold in the heat radiating up from the soil. To retain as much heat as possible, make sure the cover reaches to the ground on all sides of the plant or bed. Watering thoroughly before covering the plants may help too, since moist soil holds and releases more heat than dry soil.

Place covers over plants in late afternoon to early evening. Remove them the next morning. 🌾

HAVE ON HAND:

▶ Plastic milk jugs

▶ Scissors

▶ Stones

▶ Cardboard boxes

▶ Newspaper

▶ Floating row covers

▶ Boards

SINGLE PLANT. *Cut off the bottom of a plastic milk jug. Place jug over the plant.*

GROUPS. *Set cardboard boxes over transplants. Place stones around edges to keep them in place.*

SEEDBEDS. *Lay sheets of newspaper over seedbeds. Weight down edges with soil or rocks.*

WHOLE BEDS. *Protect beds with floating row covers. Use boards, stones, or soil to hold down edges.*

Bulbs

SPRING

Planting spring-flowering bulbs is truly an act of faith. It seems impossible that the tiny bulbs are capable of producing beautiful flowers and lush foliage. They also require patience and planning on your part, since they need to be planted months ahead of when they'll bloom. It's hard to think about daffodils and tulips in August and September, when there is so much else going on in the garden. But after a long winter, you'll be glad you made the effort when you see masses of cheerful and colorful bulbs emerging to greet the spring.

It's easy to tuck these versatile plants into all parts of your garden. Plant tulips and daffodils at the back of your perennial borders, so emerging perennials can cover up ripening bulb foliage. Combine spring bulbs with early blooming annuals, such as forget-me-nots and pansies, for a spectacular spring show. Or use later-flowering annuals to fill the spaces left when spring bulbs die back to the ground in early summer. Spring bulbs also work well interplanted with groundcovers such as common periwinkle. The bulbs provide seasonal color while the ground cover provides an attractive foundation. Container plantings let you enjoy spring bulbs either outdoors or in. ❀

FALL

Don't forget to consider summer- and fall-blooming bulbs when you plan your flower gardens. Some, such as lilies and autumn crocus, are as easy to plant as spring bulbs—plant them once and watch them multiply each year. These are known as "hardy" bulbs, since most of them can live outside through the winter. Other late bulbs, including dahlias, gladiolus, and tuberous begonias, may need to be stored indoors during the winter, depending on where you live. These "tender" bulbs may survive outside in the warmest climates, but most gardeners dig them up and replant in the spring, or else buy and plant new bulbs each year. Either way, they are still worth the little extra trouble, since tender bulbs produce some of the most spectacular flowers you can find.

Try tall bulbs, such as lilies and cannas, to add height to flower beds and borders. Plant extra dahlias and gladiolus in a separate cutting garden, so you can enjoy the luxury of freshly cut flowers without taking anything away from your regular garden display. Low-growing plants, such as tuberous begonias, are well suited to containers. Pair the shortest-growing summer and fall bulbs, including fall crocus, with ground covers for seasonal interest. ❦

Selecting Healthy Bulbs

Start with healthy, vigorous bulbs, and you are virtually guaranteed beautiful results in your garden. You'll find the best selection and quality if you shop early in the appropriate season. Spring-flowering bulbs appear in stores in early September; look for summer-blooming bulbs in early spring, and fall-flowering bulbs in July and August. Buying your bulbs soon after they arrive in the store also will keep them from drying out. If you buy through mail-order, bulbs will be shipped at the right planting time for your area.

There is an amazing variety of bulbs available. While these underground food-storage structures are generally grouped together under the term "bulbs," the only true bulbs are those with layers of food-storing leaves surrounding a central growth bud. True bulbs include daf-fodils, hyacinths, lilies, and tulips. Corms, such as crocus and gladiolus, are actually swollen stems surrounded by a papery "tunic." Dahlias grow from swollen roots joined by a bud-bearing crown. Caladiums, tuberous begonias, and other tubers produce fleshy under-ground stems with "eyes" that develop into roots or leaves and flowers. Cannas grow from rhizomes, which are thick, horizontal, underground stems.

Most bulbs are sold dry (dormant), without either roots or top growth. The largest will give the best garden display. Look for those labeled "top size" or "double-nosed." Smaller "landscape size" bulbs are less expensive, making them a good choice for naturalizing in large quantities. New bulb cultivars, or cultivated varieties, tend to cost more but aren't necessarily better than older, proven selections.

Make sure the bulbs you buy are healthy. Choose the largest and firmest specimens, with no blemishes or soft spots that might indicate disease or rot. Double bulbs are desirable and should not be separated before planting.

Early planting will give your bulbs plenty of time to form a sturdy root sys-tem before they produce leaves and flow-ers. If you must wait, store them in a cool, dry, well-ventilated place. The crisper of a refrigerator is fine for spring bulbs but too cold for summer bulbs. Store summer bulbs in a paper bag or a basket in a cool, dark corner of your basement or garage. And don't keep apples in the same drawer in which you store bulbs: apples release a gas that may be harmful to them. 🌸

Choose crocus corms that are firm and heavy for their size. Look for plump growth buds; avoid those with top growth.

Look for lily bulbs with plump, fleshy scales. Unlike most bulbs, lilies will also have fleshy roots when you buy them.

Select daffodil bulbs with intact skins that are mostly unblemished. Double-nosed bulbs produce a better show than single-nosed bulbs.

Tulip bulbs should be firm, with no signs of mold. The skin can be loose, but it should not be split or missing.

Healthy hyacinth bulbs should not have soft spots. Growth buds, if visible, should be pale and plump. Skin color depends on flower color.

Dahlia tubers should have firm, unshriveled roots without noticeable growth; there may be small buds where the roots are joined.

HERE'S HOW

RODENT-PROOF BULBS

If mice, chipmunks, and ground squirrels are a problem in your garden, plant your bulbs in buried cages made of ½-inch wire mesh.

Dig a planting area about 1 foot deep, and line the sides and bottom with wire mesh. Replace soil and plant your bulbs at the proper depth. Cover the bulbs with soil, then add a top layer of wire mesh. Make sure the top and bottom wire layers fit together closely to prevent animals from tunneling between the top or bottom and sides. A ½-inch layer of mulch will hide the wire on the soil surface.

Planting Bulbs

ONE-LAYER BEDS

Few garden plants produce as dependable a display as bulbs do for so little effort. The key to success is choosing the right planting site. Most bulbs need full sun as they grow. But once foliage dies back, the light they get is no longer important. Spring-blooming bulbs thrive under deciduous trees and shrubs, since they can get the sun they need before the leaves of larger plants block their light. Bulbs that bloom later in the season or in the fall need a site that will stay sunny through the summer.

Good soil and adequate drainage are critical for healthy bulbs; most bulbs will rot quickly in soggy soil. Loose, deep, humus-rich soil is best for vigorous growth. If your soil tends to be shallow, compacted, or poorly drained, consider planting your bulbs in raised beds.

Before planting in your prepared bed, loosen the top 1 foot of soil and work in a 2-inch layer of compost. To add bulbs to a perennial border, plant where foliage of emerging plants will cover bulb foliage by early summer.

Arrange your bulbs in clumps of five or more for larger bulbs, nine or more for smaller ones. Space large bulbs 6 inches apart, small bulbs 1 to 3 inches apart.

Fertilize each spring with a balanced organic fertilizer or a ½-inch layer of compost to provide nutrients for developing roots, then cover with a 1-inch layer of mulch. 🌿

HAVE ON HAND:

▶ Trowel or bulb planter

▶ Shovel for digging larger planting areas

▶ Water

▶ Compost or organic fertilizer

▶ Mulch

In a prepared bed, with a trowel or bulb planter, dig planting holes at depth 3 times the height of bulb.

Place bulb in hole, with the bud pointing upward. If you can't find a bud, set bulb on its side.

Fill in around bulb with soil removed from the hole. Firm the soil over the bulb with your foot.

Water deeply; add organic fertilizer or ½-inch layer of compost. Top with 1-inch layer of mulch to retain water.

MULTI-LAYERED BEDS

Planting your bulbs in layers is a great way to get a spectacular spring show of flowers in a limited space. Or, with a little planning, you can have blooms in every season.

To create a spring layered planting, start with a large-bulbed flower, such as a daffodil, hyacinth, or tulip. Then choose one with a smaller bulb, such as snowdrop, Siberian squill, Grecian windflower, or grape hyacinth. You might also include a medium-sized bulb, such as Spanish bluebell or checkered lily, for a middle layer. Mix and match bulbs in each layer, as long as each kind of bulb needs the same planting depth.

Plant your all-season display by bulb size also. For example, you might set lilies on the bottom layer (summer), tulips next (late spring), with spring Dutch crocus and showy crocus sharing the top layer (early spring and fall).

For a really finished look, consider adding ground cover over the layered bulbs. Ivy and common periwinkle offer evergreen foliage. Low-growing flowers, including primroses, forget-me-nots, and pansies also make excellent companions for bulbs.

Layered plantings use up soil nutrients more quickly than single plantings, so it's important to fertilize regularly. Apply a ½-inch layer of compost in early spring or a commercial organic fertilizer in mid-spring, following the package directions. 🌺

Dig planting hole to depth needed by larger bulbs and wide enough to hold bulbs spaced 6 inches apart.

Set bulbs in hole, buds pointing up. Gently pull soil back into hole to depth needed for next bulb.

Add layer of smaller bulbs spaced 1 to 3 inches apart, buds pointing up. Backfill the rest of hole with soil.

Firm soil; water thoroughly. Add organic fertilizer or ½-inch layer of compost. Top with 1 inch of mulch.

Naturalizing Bulbs

Bulbs can transform a boring grassy area into a carpet of colorful flowers for an unforgettable spring or fall display. The technique of planting bulbs in random, natural-looking drifts under trees and in grassy areas is known as naturalizing. It's easy to do, and the arrangement will look better each year as your bulbs multiply and spread.

Naturalizing works best in well-drained sites in open areas or under deciduous trees. Dense, vigorous turf can smother bulbs, so look for a spot where grass is on the thin side. It's also important to choose a spot that doesn't need to look perfectly groomed all the time. Spring-flowering bulbs need to keep their foliage to store nutrients for the next year's flowers. Let foliage turn yellow before cutting it down. And if you've naturalized fall-blooming bulbs, you'll need to stop mowing in late summer, when their flower buds begin to emerge from the soil.

Traditional favorites for naturalizing in grassy areas include many of the short-stemmed, small-flowered bulbs, such as spring- and fall-flowering crocuses, Grecian windflower, common snowdrops, grape hyacinths, and Siberian squill. Taller bulbs can also produce a good show. You may want to try summer snowflake, bluebells, and daffodils. Experiment with color, height, and bloom times to achieve a three-season show of bulbs. ❀

HAVE ON HAND:

▶ Trowel or bulb planter

▶ Spade

▶ Hand fork

▶ Water

LARGE. *Scatter bulbs randomly over planting area. Dig individual holes with trowel or bulb planter.*

Drop one bulb in each hole, with bud pointing upward. Replace soil and turf; firm it with your foot.

SMALL. *Cut a 16 x 18-inch "H" in grass with a spade; fold back flaps. Loosen soil with a hand fork.*

Nestle bulbs randomly into the soil. Replace grass flaps and press down firmly. Water thoroughly.

Lifting and Storing Bulbs

Hardy bulbs are tough and trouble-free. They can grow, beautiful and content, in the same spot for years. Cold-tender bulbs, however, are worth a little special care if you want them to grace your garden each year. North of Zone 9, bring gladiolus, caladiums, tuberous begonias, and dahlias indoors for the winter. Cannas can usually overwinter outdoors in Zone 8 but need indoor storage in colder areas.

Many gardeners treat tender bulbs as annuals, leaving them in the garden for the winter and buying new ones each spring. But overwintering indoors is simple, and you'll be sure to have your favorites come spring.

A little cold weather won't hurt most tender bulbs, but lift them before the ground freezes. If foliage turns yellow before frost, dig tender bulbs then. Otherwise, dig before frost is predicted, or just after bulb leaves blacken.

Storing bulbs in a dark, frost-free location (50°F is ideal) will ensure dormancy. Tender bulbs with fleshy roots, including dahlias, cannas, and tuberous begonias, are prone to drying, so bury them in barely moist vermiculite or sawdust. Label bulb containers to avoid confusion.

Each month, check your stored bulbs, discarding any that are soft or rotted. Sprinkle them with water if the roots look shriveled. Unpack in spring and plant them as you would newly purchased bulbs. ❧

HAVE ON HAND:

▶ Spading fork

▶ Pruning shears

▶ Vermiculite or sawdust

▶ Containers

▶ Plastic mesh bags

DAHLIAS. *Dig before or just after first frost. Cut stems to 6 inches. Lift roots with spading fork.*

Allow clumps to dry for a week; brush off loose soil. Store roots in vermiculite in a cool, frost-free spot.

GLADIOLUS. *Dig corms with spading fork when foliage yellows. Set in shady place to dry for a week.*

Trim tops to 1 inch. Separate new corms from base. Store corms in mesh bags in cool, frost-free spot.

Transplanting Bulbs

If your bulbs aren't exactly where you want them, don't despair—they are easy to move. The secret to successful transplanting is waiting until the bulb leaves begin to die down. Yellowing foliage is the signal that your bulbs have finished storing food for the season and are preparing to go dormant. Bulbs moved at this point will be well settled into their new spot by the time new root growth starts.

Digging a wide circle around the clump you are moving will reduce the chance of cutting into the

bulbs as you dig. If you do spear or slice any bulbs during the transplanting process, don't try to save them. Damaged bulbs are an easy target for diseases that could spread to your other bulbs.

Prepare your planting site as you would for new bulbs, and do it before you lift the bulbs to be transplanted. Loosen the soil to a depth of 6 inches for small bulbs, such as crocuses; dig 8 to 10 inches deep for tulips and daffodils, and 10 to 12 inches for lilies. Make individual holes for single bulbs, or dig larger ones for clumps.

Move dug-up bulbs to their new planting sites immediately to keep them from drying out. If you're planting a number of bulbs, lay them out before planting to achieve the desired color mix and pattern. Bulbs can be planted close together for greater impact but, to decrease chances of rot, don't let bulbs touch each other when you plant them.

HAVE ON HAND:

▶ Spading fork for large clumps

▶ Trowel or hand fork for small clumps

▶ Water

LARGE. *Once foliage yellows, use spading fork to dig a deep circle, 3 to 6 inches wider than bulb clump.*

Lift clump, using stalks as a handle, and move it to new site. Replant to same depth; water thoroughly.

SMALL. *Dig around bulbs with a hand fork or trowel. Slide your fingers under the clump to lift bulbs.*

Prepare a hole large enough to hold clump. Place clump in hole, replace soil, and water thoroughly.

Forcing Bulbs

Bring the beauty of spring into your home by growing bulbs for indoor bloom. The technique, known as forcing, lets you enjoy freshly grown flowers all winter long. Traditional favorites for forcing include small spring bulbs such as crocus, grape hyacinth, and dwarf iris. Hyacinths, daffodils, and many tulips also adapt well to this method.

For a colorful display, plant several kinds of bulbs in layers in one container. Be certain to leave enough growing room for large bulb roots (see Multi-Layered Beds, page 39).

The key to forcing bulbs is providing the right conditions for both root and top growth. Bulbs need a cool period after planting in order to establish strong root growth, followed by a cold period to ensure dormancy and then a warm, moist period to encourage growth and flowering.

Plan ahead in order to stagger bloom times for your forced bulbs. For example, tulips need 10 to 16 weeks of cold, daffodils 12 to 18 weeks, and hyacinths 6 to 10 weeks. Crocus and other small bulbs need about 8 weeks of cold. Once brought out, they will need several more weeks to grow and flower.

Keep bulbs in a cool spot with strong light to prolong flowering. After bloom, discard them, or water and fertilize regularly until leaves die down, then plant them outdoors. In a year or two they will bloom along with your other garden bulbs. 🌾

HAVE ON HAND:

▶ Container with drainage holes

▶ Potting soil

▶ Water

In late summer or early fall, add 2 inches of potting soil to a container 6 inches deep and 6 to 10 inches wide.

Add bulbs, almost touching, pointed end up. Add more soil, leaving tips uncovered. Water thoroughly.

Set in cool, dark place for 4 weeks to set roots; move to a cold frame, unheated garage, or basement.

Keep an eye on the pot and when new shoots appear, bring indoors. Set in bright place; water regularly.

A Guide to Bulbs

SPRING

Welcome spring with a bounty of beautiful spring bulbs. Try your hand with all of these traditional favorites, ideally in massed plantings, whether of one kind or the entire lot.

CROCUS
Crocus spp. and hybrids
4-6 inches tall
Zones 3-8
Purple, yellow, or white flowers; narrow green leaves; average soil; sun/partial shade. Plant 2-4 inches deep.

DAFFODILS
Narcissus spp. and hybrids
6-18 inches tall
Zones 4-8
Yellow, white, or bicolor flowers; strap-shaped green leaves; average soil; sun/partial shade. Plant 6 inches deep.

SUMMER

Mix summer-blooming bulbs with annuals and perennials to add height and color to beds and borders. Some bulbs have leaves that are as pretty as any flower.

CANNA
Canna x generalis,
2-6 feet tall
All zones
Red, pink, orange, or yellow flowers; broad green or purplish leaves; average soil; sun. Dig for winter storage north of Zone 8.

CALADIUM
Caladium x hortulanum
1-2 feet tall
All zones
Red, pink, white, and green leaves; moist soil; partial shade. Dig for winter storage north of Zone 10.

FALL

Extend the season by adding late summer, fall, and winter-blooming bulbs to your garden. Try dahlias in beds and borders; interplant others with ground cover.

AUTUMN CROCUS
Colchicum autumnale
4-6 inches tall
Zones 4-9
Rosy pink flowers; strap-like green leaves in spring; average soil; sun/partial shade. Plant 4-5 inches deep.

DAHLIA
Dahlia hybrids
1-5 feet tall
All zones
Red, pink, orange, yellow, purple, or white flowers; green or reddish leaves; average soil; sun. Plant 4 inches deep. Dig for winter north of Zone 9.

Afterbloom Care

Hardy bulbs are among the most trouble-free garden plants, but they will benefit from a little special attention. Get the best from your bulbs the following season by giving them a bit of extra care after bloom. ❧

1

Once the flowers fade, pinch or cut off the developing seed pods, unless you plan to collect seed. This is particularly important with daffodils, tulips, lilies, and other medium- to large-flowered bulbs; don't worry about crocus and other small bulbs.

TULIPS

Tulipa spp. and hybrids
6-30 inches tall
Zones 3-8
Flowers in a wide range of colors; broad green leaves; average soil; sun/partial shade. Plant 6-8 inches deep.

HYACINTH

Hyacinthus orientalis
8-12 inches tall
Zones 4-8
Blue, purple, red, pink, yellow, or white flowers; strap-shaped green leaves; average soil; sun. Plant 6 inches deep.

GRAPE HYACINTHS

Muscari spp.
6-8 inches tall
Zones 4-8
Clusters of purple-blue or white flowers; narrow green leaves; average soil; sun/partial shade. Plant 2-3 inches deep.

GLADIOLUS

Gladiolus x *hortulanus*
2-5 feet tall
All zones
Red, pink, orange, yellow, purple, or white flowers; green leaves; average soil; sun. Plant 4 inches deep. Dig for winter storage north of Zone 9.

LILY

Lilium spp. and hybrids
2-5 feet tall
Zones 4-8
Red, pink, orange, yellow, or white flowers; green leaves; average soil; sun/partial shade. Plant 6 to 8 inches deep.

TUBEROUS BEGONIA

Begonia x *tuberhybrida*
hybrids, 12-18 inches tall
All zones
Red, pink, orange, yellow, or white flowers; green leaves; moist soil; partial shade. Dig for winter storage north of Zone 10.

HARDY CYCLAMEN

Cyclamen coum
2-4 inches tall
Zones 5-9
Carmine flowers; silver-and-green leaves; winter-blooming; average soil; partial shade. Plant bulbs 1 inch deep.

ITALIAN ARUM

Arum italicum
12-18 inches tall
Zones 6-10
White flowers in spring; showy spikes of orange berries in fall; average soil; partial shade. Plant 2-3 inches deep.

SHOWY CROCUS

Crocus speciosus
4-6 inches tall
Zones 5-9
Lavender-purple flowers with deep purple veins; grassy green leaves in spring; average soil; sun. Plant 3-4 inches deep.

2 In the garden, don't be tempted to bundle or braid the bulb leaves after bloom; let them grow naturally and wait until they turn yellow to pull them up. Interplant with bushy annuals or perennials to mask declining bulb foliage.

3 If you've naturalized bulbs in grassy areas, wait until the bulb leaves have yellowed before making the first spring mowing. Keep an eye out for the buds of fall-flowering bulbs in late summer, and stop mowing as soon as they appear.

Annuals

FOR SUN

Annuals, most of them sun-loving, easy and dependable, provide months of color and fragrance at small cost with little work. You'll never tire of their variety or exhaust their usefulness.

Annuals for cutting, for example, can be planted in their own garden or toward the back of a sunny perennial bed where their cut stems will be hidden. Annuals can be grouped or scattered in beds, tucked almost anywhere, or planted in hanging baskets for instant color. To accent a sunny yard, you might choose a formal annual bed, with rows of only a few kinds or colors, or casually combine height and color to create a cheerful mix.

Annuals also complement other plants. Use sweet alyssum or dusty miller as an edging for perennial borders or shrub plantings. Add annuals to new perennial gardens to fill space while perennials get established, or where early flowering bulbs die back.

Many annuals make excellent container plants for sunny sites. Decorate your deck or patio with pots of yellow cosmos or Madagascar periwinkle. Tuck in some heliotrope or sweet alyssum for their delightful fragrance. Let petunias trail out of window boxes, or plant morning glories or scarlet runner beans for a quick and colorful summer screen. ❀

FOR SHADE

Shady gardens don't have to be green and boring; you can add sparkle with colorful, shade-appreciating annuals. There are a number of annual plants that prefer some shade, such as the dappled sun and shade created by a high tree canopy. Fragant, old-fashioned flowering tobacco is one. It appreciates partial shade so much that its flowers will fade if it is placed in full sun.

Also for partial shade areas, flowering annuals such as impatiens and wishbone flowers will brighten beds and borders all season long. A more varied look can be obtained by adding coleus or caladium (a bulb often treated as an annual) and other shade-loving foliage plants to your garden. Their unusual leaf colors, variegated leaf patterns, and plant forms can add variety and contrast to an edging of flowers and provide a backdrop for more vivid bloomers.

Container gardens filled with shade-loving annuals also make excellent accents for shady gardens—and you don't even have to do any digging. In addition, these portable gardens can be moved and rearranged as the season progresses so that they always get the right amount of shade and provide you with the best display. ❧

Selecting Healthy Annuals

To get the best possible annuals for your flower garden, you need to be a smart shopper. By taking a few minutes to look carefully at potential purchases, you can make sure that you're getting healthy, top-quality plants that will thrive when you get them home.

Start by shopping at a reputable nursery or garden center. The facility should be clean and organized, without weeds or dead plants lying around. The plants themselves should be clearly labeled, so you can be sure you're getting the ones you want. And they should be well watered, not dry or wilted. Most annuals can recover from wilting once or twice, but repeated wilting can lead to stunted growth later on.

It's also critical to check plants for pests and diseases before you buy them. After all, you don't want to bring problems home to your healthy garden. Common pests of annuals include aphids, spider mites, and whiteflies. Always inspect the leaves (both sides) and the stems, especially near the shoot tips, for signs of damage. Aphids feed on stems, leaves, buds, and flowers, causing yellowing or distorted growth. The leaves of aphid-infested plants often feel sticky, from the sugary "honeydew"

excreted by the pests as they feed. Spider mites are tiny pests that tend to feed on the undersides of leaves, producing a yellow or brown stippling on the upper leaf surfaces. You may also see tiny webs on the undersides of the leaves. Whiteflies are easy to see; just look for these small, bright white pests to fly up when you shake or brush a plant. Whiteflies usually feed on the undersides of leaves, producing stunted growth and yellowed leaves. You'll also want to avoid buying any annuals with powdery white or fuzzy gray patches on the flowers or foliage (symptoms of powdery mildew and botrytis blight).

When shopping for flowering annuals, avoid the temptation of buying plants that are in full bloom. It's fine if there are one or two flowers per plant, especially if you need to be sure you're getting a certain color. But plants not yet flowering will recover most quickly from transplanting; they can put their energy into producing new roots rather than flowers. When they start blooming, usually within 2 to 3 weeks of transplanting, the plants will have a well-established root system that can support a generous display of flowers throughout the season. 🌺

When selecting plants, choose compact, bushy, vigorous-looking plants, with top growth that is in proportion to the size of the container.

Choose plants with firm, evenly-colored leaves and stems. Avoid annuals with yellow, discolored, or limp foliage.

Check the bottom of the container for visible roots. Avoid buying annuals that have circling or matted roots, which are likely to be dried out.

On flowering annuals, choose plants with only leaves or just a few open blooms, rather than those in full flower.

Look closely at stems and at both sides of a few leaves. They should be free of holes, speckling, webbing, and other signs of insect problems.

Inspect shoot tips and buds for aphids, tiny green, black, or reddish pests, that cluster on stems. Don't buy infested plants.

HERE'S HOW

CONTROLLING SELF-SOWERS

Self-sowing annuals–those that sprout from seed from the previous year's plants–can be a bane or a boon in your garden. If you enjoy creating carefully planned annual displays or color theme gardens, self-sown plants of varying colors may pop up here and there and alter your design. If you enjoy an informal look to your beds and borders and don't mind a variety of colors and heights mingling together, allowing annuals to self-sow can provide playful and surprising results.

While it's possible for almost any annual to self-sow, exactly which ones will reseed for you depends on your particular garden conditions. A few that reseed readily in most areas include bachelor's buttons, cleome, cosmos, garden balsam, morning glory, sweet alyssum, four-o'clocks, flowering tobacco, moss rose, and nasturtiums.

To prevent annuals from self-sowing, pinch or cut off the flowers as soon as they fade and start to set seed. (This also encourages more blossoms.) Otherwise, simply allow plants to produce and drop their seed as they will.

Planting Annuals

Once you have healthy, homegrown, or purchased seedlings in hand, it's time to get your garden growing. First, make sure your annuals are properly adjusted to outdoor conditions (see Hardening Off, page 31), and danger of frost has passed. Next, you'll need a site with fertile, prepared soil (see Cultivating Your Soil, page 22).

Choose a cool, cloudy day for planting. Early evening is also a good time. Hot sun can cause transplants to wilt quickly, stressing the plants and slowing down the development of new roots. Water your annuals thoroughly before planting to minimize wilting.

Pinch off any flowers that have formed on the plants. Removing the flowers will encourage your plants to put energy into root growth, where it is truly needed. Within a few weeks, annuals treated this way will be growing and blooming vigorously, supported by a strong, spreading root system.

Take annuals out of their containers and plant them one at a time, so the roots won't be exposed to drying sun and wind. If they are growing in peat pots or pellets, simply tear off the upper rim and bottom and use a knife to cut a few slits in the sides. Space plants according to the directions on the seed packet or label. If you can't find specific recommendations, space holes at a distance of half the plant's ultimate height. Though your planting might look sparse at first, your annuals will quickly fill in the space, growing stronger and healthier than crowded plants would.

Keep annuals well watered for the first few weeks after transplanting, until the plants are well established and are producing new growth. Mulching with chopped leaves, shredded bark, or other organic material will help to keep the soil moist, as well as discourage weed seeds from sprouting around your plants. 🌺

Water your hardened-off annuals thoroughly. Pinch off any open flowers to help channel energy to roots.

Fill in around the plant's roots with soil. Gently but firmly tamp down the soil around the stem with your fingers.

HAVE ON HAND:

▶ Trowel

▶ Water

▶ Fish emulsion or seaweed extract

▶ Mulch

Use a trowel to dig individual holes in prepared soil. Space holes 6 to 12 inches apart, depending on your plant's mature height.

Remove plant from its pot or pack. Set it in the hole with the stem base, or crown, at the same depth that it was in the container.

When you are finished planting, water your annuals thoroughly. Fertilize with fish emulsion or seaweed extract.

Apply a 1- to 2-inch layer of mulch over the soil. Keep mulch at least 2 inches away from the base of the plant's stem.

HERE'S HOW

QUICK COLOR TOUCH-UPS

Flower beds are a traditional and popular way to display annual plants, but you don't have to stop there. Annuals also make ideal fillers around perennial plants, especially in new gardens where the perennials have not yet filled in. You also can plant annuals in the bare spots created when spring-flowering bulbs die back to the ground in early summer. (Dig planting holes to the side of the bulb clump, to avoid digging up or cutting into the bulbs.)

Annuals are a natural choice for container plantings, too. Growing them in pots and planters allows you to bring beautiful flowers and fragrance close to the house, brightening up decks, patios, steps, and porches. Tuck potted annuals into beds and borders to fill in gaps that have developed by mid- to late summer.

A Guide to Annuals

REDS AND PINKS

Red flowers are eye-catching in any garden. Mix them with yellow and orange flowers for a bright border or blend soft pinks with pastel flowers for a more romantic look.

COSMOS
Cosmos bipinnatus
3-4 feet tall
All zones
Red, pink, or white flowers from midsummer to frost; ferny green leaves; average to moist, well-drained soil; sun.

GERANIUM
Pelargonium x hortorum
1-2 feet tall
All zones
Red, pink, salmon, or white blooms from late spring to frost; fuzzy green leaves; average soil; sun/partial shade.

YELLOWS AND ORANGES

Yellow and orange blooms are always a cheering sight. They'll stand out from a distance, so try them in beds and borders around the edge of your property.

CALENDULA
Calendula officinalis
1-2 feet tall
All zones
Orange or yellow flowers, from summer to fall; green leaves; average soil; sun. Pinch off spent blooms.

MARIGOLD
Tagetes spp.
6-36 inches tall
All zones
Yellow, orange, maroon, or creamy white blooms from early summer to frost; ferny green leaves; average soil; sun.

BLUES AND PURPLES

Blue and purple flowers tend to blend into the background when seen from a distance. Plant them with contrasting yellows and oranges to intensify their hue.

AGERATUM
Ageratum houstonianum
6-12 inches tall
All zones
Light to deep purple-blue, pink, or white blooms from early summer to frost; average soil; sun/partial shade.

BROWALLIA
Browallia speciosa
8-18 inches tall
All zones
Blue, purple, or white flowers from summer to frost; average to moist, well-drained soil; partial shade.

Stretching the Season

Annuals are popular not only for their beauty but also for their long flowering period. Most, however, need a little help from you to bloom their best throughout the season. Try some of the easy techniques shown here to get the most from your annual beds and borders. 🌺

Interplant pansies, primroses, poppies, and other spring flowers with summer- and fall-blooming annuals such as cosmos, edging lobelia, impatiens, and scarlet sage. These later-blooming plants will start their show as spring flowers begin to fade.

IMPATIENS
Impatiens wallerana
6-24 inches tall
All zones
Red, pink, orange, lavender, or white blooms from late spring until frost; green leaves; average to moist soil; partial shade.

SCARLET SAGE
Salvia splendens
1-2 feet tall
All zones
Red, pink, salmon, deep purple, or white flowers from summer to fall; green leaves; average soil; sun.

WAX BEGONIA
Begonia semperflorens-cultorum hybrids
6-8 inches tall
All zones
Red, pink, white flowers early summer to frost; green or bronze leaves; moist, well-drained soil; partial shade.

NASTURTIUM
Tropaeolum majus
10-12 inches tall
All zones
Red, orange, or yellow flowers from early summer through fall; round green leaves; average to dry soil; sun.

SUNFLOWER
Helianthus annuus
2-8 feet tall
All zones
Maroon, yellow, orange, or bronze flowers from mid-summer to mid-fall; broad green leaves; average soil; sun.

ZINNIA
Zinnia spp.
6-36 inches tall
All zones
Red, pink, orange, yellow, green, or white flowers from early summer to frost; green leaves; average soil; sun.

EDGING LOBELIA
Lobelia erinus
6-8 inches tall
All zones
Blue, purple, or white blooms from late spring to frost; tiny green or reddish leaves; average soil; sun/partial shade.

PETUNIA
Petunia x hybrida
6-10 inches tall
All zones
Red, pink, yellow, purple, or white flowers from early summer to frost; fuzzy green leaves; average soil; sun/light shade.

WISHBONE FLOWER
Torenia fournieri
10-12 inches tall
All zones
Purplish blue flowers with yellow centers from early summer to frost; green leaves; moist, well-drained soil; partial shade.

Once a week, pinch or cut spent blooms. This technique, known as deadheading, prevents seed formation and encourages plants to flower more. Deadheading works well with many annuals, including snapdragons, cosmos, marigolds, and zinnias.

If flowering stops or slows during the dog days of summer, cut stems back by ½, add organic fertilizer, and soak the soil to encourage a new flush of growth. Try this with ageratum, edging lobelia, petunias, and sweet alyssum.

Perennials

FOR SUN

Think of perennials, and images of peonies, poppies, and phlox probably come to mind. These and other classic perennials are the stars of the sunny garden. Full-sun sites provide perfect conditions for the widest range of flowering and foliage perennials, giving you plenty of plants to choose from.

To add interest along a wall or fence, for example, plan a perennial border filled with a variety of heights and colors, such as mat-forming pinks, mounding asters, and spiky, tall irises. Or make an attractive landscape accent by creating a free-form "island" bed in part of your lawn. In either garden style, the general rule is to put the tallest plants in the back (or middle, for an island bed) and work down to the lowest plants around the edges. But it's also interesting to bring a few medium and tall plants toward the edge, to avoid creating a stair-step effect.

Full-sun sites need some special attention, however. Soil will probably dry out quickly, so you'll likely have to water more often. Working compost or other organic matter into the soil before planting will keep more moisture where the roots need it. And applying mulch over the soil after planting will help the roots stay cool and moist. 🌿

FOR SHADE

On a hot summer day, few things are more welcome than a shady glade filled with lush foliage and pale flowers. Most properties have at least one spot ideal for perennials that can't take the heat. In that area, start the season with spring-blooming perennials, such as the dainty flower sprays of barrenworts or the curious-looking hooded blooms of Jack-in-the-pulpit. For later interest, add a variety of ferns for their lovely leaves. Hostas also offer fabulous foliage, in shades of green, gold, and dusty blue, often edged or striped with cream or white. Their purple, lavender, or white summer flowers are an added bonus.

Shady spots often tend to be on the moist side, since they are more sheltered from drying sun and wind. If your shady site has evenly moist soil, you will want to include plants that thrive in those conditions, including ferns, astilbes and primroses. If your site tends to be dry (possibly due to the thirsty roots of nearby trees and shrubs), work compost or other organic matter into the soil as you dig. Water regularly for the first month or two after planting to help your new shade-loving selections get established. Then, water only as needed during spells of dry weather.

Selecting Healthy Perennials

Successful perennial gardens begin with healthy, vigorous plants. You'll want to check each potential purchase carefully to make sure you are getting the best-quality plants for your money.

Shop at a reputable supplier. Ask gardening friends and neighbors about their good and bad experiences with perennial plant sources, and find out which places they recommend. Nurseries and garden centers with display gardens are helpful, since you can see how the plants will perform in your particular area. If the perennials are thriving there, chances are good that they are well adapted to your area's climate and weather conditions.

Clearly labeled displays and plants are more than just a bonus, they are critical if you are looking for perennials with particular colors, heights, or habits. You want to buy your plants while they are still young and leafy, since full-grown perennials will be slow to become established in your garden after planting. Useful labels will tell you what color the flowers should be and what height the plant should reach when mature.

Mid-spring is the ideal time to start shopping for perennials. By then, the plants will have started growing, but they will still be young enough to adjust easily to your garden and produce a good display the same year. Toward the end of the season plants may be on sale, but the selection will be greatly reduced and the plants may have overgrown their containers. Big plants in small pots tend to dry out quickly and may have wilted often, stressing the plant and leading to poor growth after planting.

Healthy perennials will have lush, unblemished foliage. Yellowed or discolored leaves may indicate a nutrient deficiency or disease. (Some perennials do have unusual foliage color or markings, so it's important to check the label or ask the supplier if you're not sure whether or not there's a problem.) When you inspect the plants for signs of pest problems, make sure you look at the undersides of the leaves—pests often hide there. Do not buy perennials with visible pests or signs of pest or disease damage, even at a reduced price.

If you buy from a mail-order nursery, your plants will either be coming out of dormancy (spring) or going into it (fall). Woody shrubs and trees are also perennials and are usually shipped bare-root. They may not look impressive at first but will survive if handled properly (see Here's How, page 59). (see Here's How, page 59).

Shop at a reputable nursery or garden center. Look for clean, weed-free displays and well-labeled plants.

Inspect leaves for holes, speckling, insect webbing, discoloration, malformation, and other signs of pest and disease problems.

Choose perennials that are bushy and vigorous, with top growth that's in proportion to the size of the container they are in.

Look for plants that have leaves only, or a few buds at most. Plants in full bloom will not have energy for rooting.

Make sure stems are firm and evenly colored, especially where they enter the soil; discolored stems, such as those shown here, may have rot.

Slide the perennial out of its pot so you can get a good look at the rootball. Avoid buying plants with matted or circling roots.

HERE'S HOW

SMART SHOPPING

Buying perennials can be an expensive proposition, especially if you need enough to fill a new garden. But with a few smart shopping strategies, you can get healthy, good-looking plants without breaking your budget.

Whenever possible, plan your garden a few months to a year before you are actually ready to plant, then begin shopping right away. Purchase full-looking pots, with large plants that have multiple stems. These bigger perennials will be more expensive, but you'll need only a few of each. When you get home, divide the clumps and plant the divisions in an out-of-the-way bed where they can grow and develop. By the time you are ready to transplant them to your new garden, you will have three or more good-sized perennials for the price of one.

If you want to get a new garden started immediately, consider buying small plants in 4- to 6-inch pots. They will catch up to larger plants within a year or two, and you'll have saved yourself some money in the meantime. If the garden looks a little sparse after planting, tuck in some annuals to fill the gaps while the perennials get established.

Planting Perennials

Perennials are likely to live in the same place for several years, so it's important to get them off to a great start with proper planting. First, prepare a fertile planting site (see Cultivating Your Soil, page 22). Once the site is ready, gather your plants and materials.

You can plant container-grown perennials any time the ground isn't frozen; spring and fall are ideal, since there tends to be adequate rainfall and temperatures are moderate. Hot sun can quickly cause new plants to wilt, so plant on a cool, cloudy day or in the early evening.

Watering your pots before planting will help the perennials handle trans-

planting with minimal stress. To make sure the soil is thoroughly moistened, irrigate until water runs out the bottom of the pot. Or, if the soil is very dry, set the pot in a container of water for an hour before planting to make sure the plants absorb all the water they can hold. While the perennials are still in their containers, set them out on the prepared soil, according to your garden design. Space them based on their mature spread, so that the edges of the plants will just touch when they are full grown. For example, if the plants have a 1-foot spread, space them 10 to 12 inches apart. (To find the mature spread, check the plant label or refer to an encyclopedia of perennial plants.) Make any needed adjustments to the plant arrangement before digging the planting holes.

Take the perennials out of their containers one at a time and plant them immediately, to avoid exposing the roots to drying sun and wind. Keep the plants well watered for the first few weeks after transplanting, until they are established and producing new growth. Mulch with shredded bark, chopped leaves, or other organic material to keep the soil evenly moist, encourage good root growth, and discourage weeds. 🌸

Preferably on an overcast day in spring or fall, thoroughly water perennial containers and arrange the plants in your garden.

Backfill the soil around the roots. Use your fingertips to gently but firmly press down the soil around the stem.

HAVE ON HAND:

▶ Water

▶ Trowel or shovel

▶ Fish emulsion or seaweed extract

▶ Mulch

Dig planting holes in prepared soil with a trowel or shovel. Space holes according to mature spread of each plant.

Gently slide plant out of its pot; loosen roots with your fingers. Set plant in hole carefully, so that stem base is at the same level as in the pot.

After planting the bed, water the soil thoroughly. Fertilize the entire planting with fish emulsion or seaweed extract.

Spread a 2-inch layer of mulch over the soil. Keep mulch at least 2 inches away from the base of the stem of each plant to prevent rot.

HERE'S HOW

PLANTING BARE-ROOT PERENNIALS

If you buy perennials through a mail-order nursery catalog, they may arrive bare-root—with packing but no soil around the roots. Bare-root perennials will adapt well in your garden if you give them special care at planting time. First, remove the packing material, then prune off any broken or damaged roots. Soak the remaining roots in lukewarm water for an hour or two before planting. Dig planting holes before removing the perennials from the water. Make the holes large enough to hold the roots comfortably without bending them. Then replace some soil in the center of each hole to create a cone. The top of the cone should be just even with the soil surface.

Plant bare-root perennials one at a time, setting the plant on the peak of the cone and spreading the roots out evenly over the sides. Fill in around the roots with soil, and firm the soil around the base of the plant. After planting, water thoroughly, fertilize with fish emulsion or seaweed extract, and mulch. Keep the soil evenly moist for the first 4 to 6 weeks, until plants become established and produce new growth.

Protecting Tender Perennials

Perennials are plants that live longer than two years. Not all perennials, however, can survive a harsh winter outdoors. Tender perennials, those requiring special protection from northern winters include zonal geraniums, wax begonias, impatiens, coleus, heliotrope, and browallia.

Many gardeners grow these plants as annuals, buying new ones each spring and pulling them out during fall cleanup. But you can bring your favorite tender perennials indoors in the fall and plant them in your garden again in spring. You'll get a better flower or foliage display more quickly, since overwintered plants tend to be larger than newly purchased transplants.

Three weeks before you bring a plant indoors, treat it preventively for aphids and whiteflies by spraying with insecticidal soap. Repeat a few times before digging plant up. Destroy plants that show signs of pest damage such as distorted growth, speckling, or yellowing.

During the winter, grow tender perennials in a warm, sunny window or under fluorescent plant lights. Water as needed to keep the soil evenly moist. Fertilize with a liquid organic fertilizer, such as fish emulsion. In late spring, when the danger of frost has passed, gradually move plants back outdoors (see Hardening Off, page 31). When your plants are again adjusted to the outdoors, plant them in the garden. ❦

HAVE ON HAND:

- ▶ Insecticidal soap
- ▶ Trowel
- ▶ Pots, 6 to 8 inch
- ▶ Potting soil
- ▶ Water
- ▶ Pruning shears
- ▶ Fish emulsion

In late summer, determine which plants to overwinter indoors. Pick those that are the most healthy.

In early fall, dig up small clumps of plants; plant in 6- to 8-inch pots filled with potting soil; water well.

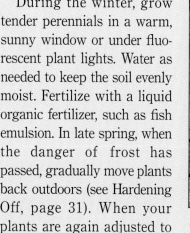

Cut stems back by half. Feed with fish emulsion. Set in shade; bring indoors before the first frost.

For plants too large to move, take cuttings from stem tips in late summer to grow indoors over winter.

Transplanting Perennials

Even the best-planned perennial garden needs a bit of fine-tuning now and then. Perhaps two flowers next to each other don't harmonize well, or two plants that would make great companions are at separate ends of the garden. Fortunately, it's easy to move most perennial plants. You can adjust your plantings until you are satisfied with the results.

The best time to transplant perennials is when they are dormant or just beginning new growth. For most, early spring is ideal. Perennials that bloom in spring adapt well to transplanting either after flowering or in the fall. If you must move your perennials during the growing season, cut their foliage back by 1/2 to 2/3 to reduce moisture loss, and water them regularly. Prepare the new planting site before digging perennials, so you can replant them immediately without their root systems drying out.

Of course, there are some perennials that don't take kindly to transplanting. Peonies, for example, may take a year or two to adjust to their new site and bloom after being moved. Those that are tap-rooted, with a single, vertical root, such as butterfly weed and gas plant, can also be tricky. If you must transplant them, dig deeply around the crown to secure as much of the main root as possible. Don't move Oriental poppies when their foliage is visible. Keep the soil moist after planting to encourage root growth. 🌸

Use a spade or trowel to cut a circle around plant, 6 inches or more away from stems and as deep.

Pry clump out of soil with a hand fork or spading fork. Keep as much soil around roots as possible.

Place clump in planting hole, with crown at level of soil surface. Fill hole around roots with soil.

Firm soil around crown. Water thoroughly. Add a 2-inch layer of mulch; avoid piling it against the crown.

A Guide to Perennials

SPRING

Celebrate spring with a planting of early-blooming perennials. Pair them with later-blooming perennials, annuals, and bulbs to extend display through the season.

COLUMBINE
Aquilegia **spp. and hybrids**
2-3 feet tall
Zones 3-9
Red, pink, yellow, purple, blue, white, or bicolor flowers; blue-green leaves; average soil; sun/partial shade.

BLEEDING HEART
Dicentra spectabilis
2-3 feet tall
Zones 3-9
Pink-and-white flowers; deeply divided, blue-green leaves; evenly moist, well-drained soil; partial shade.

SUMMER

Summer heat doesn't have to stop your garden. Keep the excitement going with a variety of dependable, easy-care flowering and foliage perennials for summer-long color.

HOSTA
Hosta **spp.**
6-36 inches tall
Zones 3-8
Purple, lavender, or white flowers; green leaves often striped with yellow or white; average soil; partial/full shade.

SHASTA DAISY
Chrysanthemum **x** *superbum*
1-3 feet tall
Zones 3-10
White flowers with yellow centers; deep green, toothed leaves; average soil; sun. Deadhead to prolong bloom.

FALL

End the season with a burst of color from late-blooming perennials interplanted with autumn-flowering bulbs and ornamental grasses for a fabulous fall display.

ASTER
Aster **spp.**
3-6 feet tall
Zones 3-8
Blue, purple, pink, or white flowers; narrow green leaves; moist, well-drained soil; sun/light shade.

CHRYSANTHEMUM
Chrysanthemum **x** *morifolium*
1-3 feet tall
Zones 3-9
Red, pink, orange, yellow, lavender, or white flowers; lobed green leaves; average soil; sun/light shade.

Controlling Invasive Perennials

Vigorous, fast-spreading perennials are excellent for filling empty spaces in the garden, but they can quickly spread out of their allotted space if you don't take steps to control them. The proper control technique depends on whether the plant spreads mainly by seed or by aboveground or belowground runners.

Some perennials, including coneflowers, feverfew, and some ornamental grasses, can become weedy as they produce many unwanted seedlings. Prevent this problem by cutting off spent flowers before they set seed.

LUNGWORT
Pulmonaria spp.
12-18 inches tall
Zones 3-8
Pink, blue, or white blooms; fuzzy green leaves, often with silver spots; moist soil; partial/full shade.

CANDYTUFT
Iberis sempervirens
6-12 inches tall
Zones 3-9
White flowers; evergreen leaves; average soil; sun/light shade. Shear spent flowers for additional bloom.

PEONY
Paeonia lactiflora
2-3 feet tall
Zones 3-8
Red, pink, or white flowers; green leaves take on reddish tints in fall; moist, well-drained soil; sun/light shade.

HARDY GERANIUM
Geranium spp.
12-18 inches tall
Zones 4-8
Pink, purple, blue, magenta, or white flowers; lobed green leaves; evenly moist soil; sun/partial shade.

BORDER PHLOX
Phlox spp.
3-4 feet tall
Zones 3-8
Red, pink, purple, or white blooms; narrow green leaves; moist, well-drained soil; sun/light shade.

DAYLILY
Hemerocallis hybrids
1-5 feet tall
Zones 3-9
Red, pink, orange, yellow, lavender, or white flowers; strap-like green leaves; average to moist soil; sun/light shade.

JAPANESE ANEMONE
Anemone x hybrida
3-5 feet tall
Zones 5-8
White or pink flowers; broad, dark green leaves; evenly moist soil with added organic matter; sun/light shade.

PLUMBAGO
Ceratostigma plumbaginoides
6-12 inches tall
Zones 5-9
Deep blue flowers; green leaves turn reddish orange in fall; average to moist soil; sun/partial shade.

SHOWY STONECROP
Sedum spectabile
18-24 inches tall
Zones 3-9
Light to dark pink blooms age to rusty red; succulent blue-green leaves; average soil; sun. Drought-tolerant.

Ajugas, bee balm, and lamb's ears are a few of the perennials that spread by runners. To control their spread, dig them up and divide the clumps every other year. Replant a few pieces; give away or discard the rest.

Root barriers can contain runner-producing perennials. Surround individual plants with plastic or metal strips that extend 2 to 3 inches above and below the soil. Or plant them in large, bottomless buckets or plastic tubs sunk into the ground and filled with soil.

Climbing Vines

ANNUAL

Annual vines have an amazing will to grow. Some mature from a small, spring-sown seed into stems that reach 20 feet by the first fall frost. This trait makes them indispensable for any site needing shade or screening in a hurry. They're a good choice, too, if pruning and maintenance are not part of your schedule. And, if you're undecided about how a perennial vine might work in a certain space, you can try an annual before making a more permanent choice.

Annual vines usually climb by wrapping their stems or tendrils around a support, so provide them with something to hold onto: netting, stakes, lattice, a trellis, or a chain-link fence. These vines grow fast—put your support in place before you plant! Once they reach the support, your vines will grab on and head for the sky with little help from you.

Use morning glories to dress up a lamppost or fence; scarlet runner beans for garden accents. Hyacinth bean will provide a curtain of leaves and flowers for a porch or patio. Adorn a deck with annual vines such as climbing nasturtiums grown in pots with either a trellis for each pot or deck railings as support. Your annual vines will provide a wealth of beautiful flowers you don't even have to stoop to admire. 🌿

PERENNIAL

What is more charming than a rustic rail fence smothered in a froth of sweet autumn clematis flowers? Or a pretty pergola covered with the purple or white flower chains of wisteria? Perennial climbers add a touch of romance to any garden.

Perennial climbers are practical, too. You can train them on permanent trellises to block unattractive views or provide privacy for outdoor entertaining. Grown on walls, they hide awkward architectural features. Use them to cover free-standing screens separating different parts of your yard, or to soften the look of a newly installed fence. Some vines, including clematis, make excellent partners for roses and shrubs, providing extra flowers in the same area without taking up additional space in the garden.

Perennial vines usually have woody stems and can grow substantially in one season—they normally need sturdy support. Some, such as Boston ivy and Virginia creeper, cling to walls without additional help. Others, including honeysuckle, clematis, and passionflowers, require something to wrap around, and may need guidance to get started in the right direction. Once they get going, however, your perennial climbers will provide years of easy-care beauty. 🌸

Selecting Healthy Climbing Vines

Starting with vigorous, pest-free plants will virtually guarantee your success with vines. They will live for many years once established, so it's worth taking a little time to make sure you get the best-quality climbers for your money.

Shop for vines at a reputable nursery or garden center. It is important that the plants be clearly labeled—especially if you are looking for a particular flower color and the plant is not yet in bloom. You can buy and plant container-grown vines any time during the growing season, but keep in mind that they'll settle in most quickly in fall or early spring.

Young vines are generally a better buy than older, larger plants. Since they grow so quickly, young vine plants will catch up to older ones in a relatively short time—usually within a season or two. Young vines will also be less expensive. And because the plants themselves are smaller, they are easier to handle and there is less chance of damaging their top growth during planting.

Before buying any vine, make sure you know how big it will be at maturity. To cover a small trellis or post, look for a relatively restrained vine, such as most varieties of clematis and honeysuckles. Extra-vigorous vines, such as wisteria

and trumpet vine, will need a sturdy arbor or fence to support them.

When you find a climber you absolutely must have, be prepared to provide the right kind of support for it. Keep in mind that the support you choose will have to be cleaned and maintained periodically, which can be hard to do when there are vines permanently attached. Consider the benefits of redwood and cedar; both are sturdy and rot-resistant. In any case, you'll want your vine to match its support in terms of both strengh and look (see Here's How). Inquire at your local nursery if you need advice or additional information.

Healthy climbers will have lush, unblemished foliage and sturdy stems. It's a plus if there is a stake or small trellis in the pot to support the developing shoots and prevent them from breaking during transit. Check the stems, shoot tips, and leaves (both sides) carefully for insects and signs of pest and disease problems, such as crinkled or discolored growth. Don't buy any vine with visible insects or disease damage, even at a bargain price. Your new plant—even with tender loving care—might be permanently weak or stunted, and your healthy garden will be at risk. ✺

Before you shop, decide on your planting location. Research vines that thrive in the conditions provided and take a list with you to the nursery.

Inspect the vine leaves for holes, discoloration, speckling or webbing, and other signs of pest and disease problems.

Choose vines that appear to be vigorous and healthy. The top growth should be in proportion to the container, neither skimpy nor too lush.

Select vines that have more than one stem per pot. Don't choose vines that are stressed at the base from bending.

Make sure the vine's stems are firm and evenly colored, especially at the base. Discolored stems may be a sign of disease.

Slide the vine out of its pot to inspect the rootball. Do not buy plants with heavily matted or circling roots.

HERE'S HOW

MATCHING VINES TO YOUR STRUCTURES

It is vital to match the habit of any vine with the support structure you have available. Bear in mind that mature vines can get heavy, so be sure your structure is strong enough to hold the vine at its mature size.

Clinging vines, such as Boston ivy and Virginia creeper, fasten themselves to a support by producing rootlets or disks along the stems. These self-clingers are easy to grow on solid structures such as stone or other kinds of walls but may damage mortar or siding. Virginia creeper does well on fences, trees, trellises.

Twining climbers, including honeysuckle, morning glory, and wisteria, pull themselves up by wrapping their stems around a support; wires or posts, for example.

Passionflower and other tendril climbers produce small, coiling stems at the leaf tips. They need a thin support to wrap around, such as wire, a chain-link fence, or plastic netting.

Planting Climbing Vines

Container-grown climbers are tough and adaptable, so you can add them to your garden any time during the growing season. Spring and fall are ideal, however, since the plants will develop a more spreading root system during cool, moist weather.

Before planting, make sure the appropriate support is painted or stained and in place for your new vine. If you attempt to install a support structure later, you risk damaging the plant's root system. Once they are planted and established, new vines will grow quickly.

Thoroughly watering the rootball before planting will help your vines handle transplanting with minimal stress. After you transplant, keep vines well watered for a few weeks, until they produce new growth. Spread a 2-inch layer of an organic mulch to help the soil stay moist and cool. Keep the mulch at least 2 inches from the stems in order to prevent rot.

As the vine stems grow, direct them to their support. Ivy and other clinging vines may take a season or two to get established and start climbing. Gently tie the stems of other climbers to the support. Guide them by inserting one or more stakes next to the rootball, angled toward the support. Use soft string or strips of cloth to loosely fasten the stems to the stakes. As the stems elongate, tie them every 6 to 12 inches, until they start grasping the support on their own. 🌺

HAVE ON HAND:

▶ Trowel or shovel

▶ Water

▶ Mulch

▶ Fish emulsion or seaweed extract

Dig a hole 6 inches wider than pot and the same depth. Dig center of hole 12 to 18 inches from support.

Water container soil thoroughly. Slide the plant out of its pot; loosen the outer roots with your fingers.

Set the plant in the hole, with its stems angled toward the support. Replace soil around the rootball.

Water, mulch, and feed with fish emulsion. Gently guide stems in the direction of the new support.

Transplanting Climbing Vines

Vines are gratifyingly easy to move. These tough, vigorous plants may take a season or two to rebloom after transplanting, but they'll readily produce new growth once they have settled into their new site.

Climbers ideally should be transplanted in late winter or early spring, after the ground has thawed. Before digging up and moving any vine, have the new trellis, post, or other support in place. This way the root system won't be disturbed again when the support is installed.

When digging a planting hole for your vine, make the center of the hole 18 inches from the support base. By not planting directly at the support's bottom, you'll have room to work around the structure (for painting or other maintenance) without damaging stems.

In general, the planting hole should be deep enough so that stems emerge from the ground at the same level they did before. Clematis is an exception. You can set the rootball 1 to 2 inches deeper. Then, if aboveground stems are killed back by a disease called clematis wilt, the plant may be able to produce new shoots from underground. Keep mulch away from stems to prevent rot.

When new growth begins to emerge, select four to six strong shoots to train toward the support and prune out the rest. Be aware that any vines that bloom only on old wood will not flower until the following year. 🌸

HAVE ON HAND:

▶ Spade or shovel
▶ Pruning shears
▶ Spading fork
▶ Tarp
▶ Water
▶ Mulch
▶ Ties for support
Optional
▶ Stakes

Install new support. Dig hole with center 18 inches from support base, 18 inches wide by 12 inches deep.

Cut stems to 1 foot or remove from old support. Dig around vine to loosen roots. Lift with spading fork.

Set rootball on tarp to move. Place plant in new hole, stems toward support, set at previous soil level.

Replace soil; water and mulch. Attach stems to support, or insert stakes to guide new shoots.

A Guide to Climbing Vines

ANNUAL FLOWERING VINES

Fast-growing annual vines are ideal for training on trellises for shade or privacy. Or grow them on a tripod of sturdy stakes for summer-to-fall flowers in beds and borders.

CRIMSON STARGLORY
Mina lobata
To 20 feet tall
All zones
Orange and yellow flowers through summer; lobed green leaves; twining stems; average soil; sun/light shade.

HYACINTH BEAN
Dolichos lablab
To 15 feet tall
All zones
Pinkish purple flowers through summer; purple seed pods in fall; green or purple leaves; twining stems; average soil; sun.

PERENNIAL FLOWERING VINES

Most perennial vines tend to be vigorous; make sure you give them sturdy support. Hybrid clematis can be trained over shrubs or roses for an interesting effect.

BLUE PASSIONFLOWER
Passiflora caerulea
To 12 feet tall
Zones 7-10
Blue-and-white flowers in summer; lobed green leaves; climbs by tendrils; average soil; sun/light shade.

CLEMATIS
Clematis spp. and hybrids
To 15 feet tall
Zones 5-9
White, pink, red, or purple blooms in spring, summer, or fall; green leaves; twining leaf stalks; moist, well-drained soil; sun.

PERENNIAL FOLIAGE VINES

For shade or privacy, try a fast-growing foliage vine on an arbor, trellis, or pergola. Clinging foliage vines, such as Boston or English ivy, look great on walls and fences.

BOSTON IVY
Parthenocissus tricuspidata
To 60 feet tall
Zones 4-10
Three-lobed, green, deciduous leaves that turn red in fall; clinging stems; average soil; sun/light shade.

BIGLEAF WINTERCREEPER
Euonymus fortunei
To 40 feet long
Zones 5-9
Glossy, evergreen leaves; small flowers and fruit whose seeds turns orange in fall; clinging; average soil; shade. Grown as bush or vine.

Invading the Landscape

Vines can be a beautiful and versatile addition to your garden, but beware—some are just too vigorous for most situations. Those that spread by underground runners, self-sown seeds, or rooting stems can become a real maintenance headache. If you have a problem vine in your yard, dig it out if possible, smother it with a heavy plastic or cardboard mulch, or cut it to the ground every two weeks until it stops resprouting. ❦

Morning glories, tender perennials often grown as decorative annuals, are noninvasive in cool climates. Where winters are warm, however, they don't die down and may self-sow more freely than you want. Check with your local nursery before you plant them.

MOONFLOWER
Calonyction aculeatum
To 15 feet tall
All zones
Fragrant, white, night-blooming flowers through summer; broad, green leaves; twining stems; average soil; sun.

MORNING GLORY
Ipomoea spp. tricolor
To 15 feet tall
All zones
White, pink, red, or blue flowers through summer; heart-shaped, green leaves; twining stems; average to dry soil; sun.

SCARLET RUNNER BEAN
Phaseolus coccineus
To 8 feet tall
All zones
Orange-red flowers from midsummer to frost; broad, green leaves; twining stems; average soil; sun.

HONEYSUCKLE
Lonicera spp.
To 30 feet tall
Zones 4-9
Orange- or red-and-yellow, summer flowers; blue-green leaves; twining stems; moist, well-drained soil; sun/partial shade.

TRUMPET VINE
Campsis radicans
To 40 feet tall
Zones 4-9
Orange or red summer flowers; green leaves with many leaflets; clinging stems; average soil; sun. Very vigorous.

WISTERIA
Wisteria floribunda
To 50 feet tall
Zones 4-10
Purple, lavender, or white flowers in late spring; deciduous green leaves; twining stems; average soil; sun/light shade.

DUTCHMAN'S PIPE
Aristolochia macrophylla
To 30 feet tall
Zones 4-8
Heart-shaped, green, deciduous leaves; twining stems; average soil; sun/partial shade. Unusual early summer flowers.

HARDY KIWI
Actinidia kolomikta
To 20 feet tall
Zones 4-10
Heart-shaped, green-, pink-and-white, deciduous leaves; twining stems; moist soil; sun/partial shade.

ENGLISH IVY
Hedera helix
To 40 feet tall
Zones 5-10
Lobed, green or variegated, evergreen leaves; clinging stems; average soil; partial/dense shade.

Japanese honeysuckle is a deciduous or semi-evergreen twining vine with white to yellow summer flowers followed by black berries. It spreads by seed and by stems that root aggressively where they touch the ground. Wiser not to plant at all.

Algerian ivy, an extremely vigorous half-hardy climber and spreader, can cover the ground with large, shiny leaves, making it impossible for anything else to grow. It also builds up thick mats of stems that provide a haven for rodents and other pests. Difficult to eradicate.

Shrubs

DECIDUOUS

Few things will accomplish as much in your garden as carefully chosen shrubs. Flowering deciduous shrubs, for example, can do many jobs: separate different parts of your yard, provide shelter and privacy, and liven up dull buildings and fences, just to name a few. A tough-to-mow slope will turn into an asset with a mass planting of low-growers such as rockspray cotoneaster. In addition to their practical benefits, flowering shrubs also offer beauty: colorful blooms as well as height and form for you to enjoy. You may want to choose one that is especially beautiful—perhaps a spirea or viburnum—as a specimen plant for accent.

The options for using flowering shrubs are limitless. Try grouping several of different sizes for the effect of a traditional flower bed with minimal work. Or plant a combination of shrubs and perennials to provide varied interest all year. Some flowering shrubs, such as winterberry hollies and viburnum, offer a display of colorful fruit well into winter. Others, including hydrangeas, have flowers or seed heads that persist for months. And, you won't be alone in your appreciation of flowering and fruiting shrubs; they also provide food and shelter for birds and other wildlife. ❧

EVERGREEN

Evergreen shrubs are often over-looked in the garden, but that is the way it is supposed to be. Their quiet greens blend into the background, making them excellent for dividing areas without drawing attention to the boundaries themselves. They make wonderful backdrops for flower gardens, their dark foliage providing a pleasing contrast to bright blooms.

Because they keep their foliage all year, tall evergreens make a good screen to shield out unattractive views. They also filter noise and wind, important if your garden is near a street or exposed to strong winds. You can shape them or enjoy their natural beauty. Low-growing types, such as creeping juniper, are well suited for use as ground covers. Use them also along paths, to keep visitors on the walkways and subtly head them in the right direction.

Some evergreen shrubs offer more than green leaves. Camellias, rhododendrons, and mountain laurel also produce colorful flowers, while many hollies have brightly colored berries. Consider planting these in masses, where they can really show off. Some needle-leaved evergreens, including junipers, are available with golden or silvery blue leaves as well as the more common green. 🌸

Selecting Healthy Shrubs

Shrubs will most likely be a permanent addition to your garden, so take some time to consider your requirements, and make sure you start with the best plants possible. A smart shopping strategy will help you select the right shrubs for your needs and conditions.

First, decide where on your property they will be planted. This is a good time to consult your garden map (see Making a Garden Map, page 8). Next, make sure you know what you are looking for. Check catalogs and gardening books or talk to salespeople at local nurseries and garden centers to find out which shrubs are well adapted to your site conditions and the mature height and spread of each shrub. While they may look small and manageable in a pot, shrubs can quickly overgrow their spot if not given enough room. Start by selecting a shrub that will fit in the space you have available in order to save yourself a lot of pruning and maintenance later on.

Since spring and fall are ideal shrub planting times, they're also good shopping times. You will generally find the widest selection in the spring. In addition to container-grown shrubs, some nurseries and garden centers offer balled-and-burlapped (B-and-B) plants in fall or early spring. These shrubs have been grown in a field, then dug up with soil around the roots; the rootball is then wrapped in burlap or plastic material. If you choose a balled-and-burlapped shrub, make sure the wrapping is evenly distributed around the rootball and secure. Exposed roots can dry out quickly and may not transplant well.

For any type of shrub, shop at a supplier with clean, well-organized displays and clearly labeled plants. Good labels will tell you about the shrub's flower color or other special features, as well as its size and preferred growing conditions, so you can make sure you are getting exactly what you want.

Healthy shrubs will have unblemished, evenly colored foliage. Yellowed or discolored leaves may indicate a nutrient deficiency or disease problem. When you check for signs of pest problems, make sure you look at the undersides of the leaves, too; pests often like to hide there. Avoid plants with fragile stems, an indication that the plant may not have been properly cared for. Also, avoid plants that have excessively twiggy growth. Both plants with fragile growth and those with very twiggy growth will be slow to establish. 🌸

Research shrubs in early spring or fall. Identify species that will adequately fill your space and thrive in the intended location.

Check the leaves for holes, speckling, insect webbing, discoloration, and other signs of disease and pest problems.

Choose shrubs with well-branched and balanced top growth that is in proportion to the size of the plant's rootball.

Select plants with plump buds and firm, vigorous stems. Avoid those with broken, shriveled, or damaged stems.

If possible, slide the shrub out of its pot so you can inspect the rootball, or ask to see it. Reject those plants with thickly matted or circling roots.

On balled-and-burlapped shrubs, make sure that the wrapping is intact, and the rootball is firm and moist.

HERE'S HOW

AVOIDING INVASIVE SHRUBS

While most shrubs are welcomed into the garden, a few may be more of a problem than a pleasure. Some barberies, for instance, reseed readily, producing many young plants throughout your garden. Other self-sowing shrubs include the multiflora rose and the butterfly bush.

Spreading shrubs can be a problem also, especially if you have a small garden. Sumacs, for example, send out underground runners (suckers), so new plants may pop up several feet from the base of the parent plant.

To avoid introducing potential problems into your garden, make sure you know what you are buying. If you aren't familiar with how a particular shrub grows, do a little research before you buy it. Visit a local botanical garden or arboretum to see firsthand how an established specimen will behave in a garden setting. If possible, talk to the staff members who maintain the plants to find out if they have any problems to report. You may still decide that you like the shrub well enough to deal with its seedlings or suckers, but at least you'll know what to expect.

Planting Shrubs

Shrubs are usually planted to grow in one spot for many years, so proper planting is an important step in helping them live a long, healthy life. Early spring is the ideal planting time, for less over-winter loss, although, with care, container-grown shrubs may be planted any time the ground isn't frozen.

If you have several shrubs to plant in one area, consider preparing a large planting bed rather than digging many individual holes (see Cultivating Your Soil, page 22). For a single shrub, a broad but fairly shallow hole (just deep enough to hold the rootball) is suffi-cient. To check the depth of the hole, measure the distance from the ground to the top of the rootball. Then lay a stake across the planting hole. Measure from the stake to the bottom of the hole. When the measurements match, the hole is the right depth.

Thoroughly water the rootball before planting to help your shrubs survive transplanting with minimal stress. Add water until it runs out of the bottom of the rootball.

Set the plant so that it is straight in the hole. For balled-and-burlapped plants, remove the binding ropes and any nails or plastic. Then cut away as much of the wrapping as you can without breaking up the rootball. Remove wire or plastic labels attached to the plant, to prevent them from cutting into the growing stems.

Water regularly and deeply, especially during dry spells. Mulch with shredded bark or chopped leaves to keep the soil moist and cool. 🌼

HAVE ON HAND:

▶ Water

▶ Shovel

▶ Mulch

Water rootball thoroughly. Dig a planting hole the same depth and twice as wide as the rootball.

If the shrub is in a container, remove the pot and loosen the outside of the rootball with your fingers.

Set shrub in the center of the hole. Remove any wrapping around the rootball. Backfill with soil.

Firm soil around stems with your foot; water. Add 2 inches of mulch; keep it 4 inches away from stems.

Transplanting Shrubs

Perhaps your shrubs have overgrown their present home, or you're planning a garden redesign. Either way, you won't have to give them up. Small shrubs are easy to transplant and will settle quickly into a new site. Established shrubs are more work to dig up and can be heavy to move; have a helper ready to carry your shrub to its new planting site.

Early to mid-fall is an ideal time to move shrubs. The air is cool but soil is still warm, providing good conditions for new root growth while discouraging energy-sapping top growth. Transplant in early spring as a second choice.

To make your job easier, tie the tops of long-stemmed shrubs with twine before digging them up. Use pruning shears or loppers to cut large roots that you can't sever cleanly with your spade.

After transplanting, untie top growth, and prune damaged stems. To prevent winter drying, protect shrubs moved in fall (especially evergreens) with a burlap or plastic mesh screen, or spray leaves with an antidesiccant to prevent moisture loss.

Regular watering during the first growing season after transplanting is critical to help your shrub settle into its new site. Water to keep soil moist if rainfall is sparse.

Fertilize transplanted shrubs in the spring. Pull back the mulch layer, scatter a balanced organic fertilizer or a 1-inch layer of compost, and replace the mulch.

HAVE ON HAND:

▶ Spade

▶ Spading fork

▶ Tarp

▶ Twine

▶ Water

▶ Mulch

Use spade to cut circle around outer spread of branches. Following circle, dig trench about 1 foot deep.

Loosen soil around rootball with spading fork. Cut roots at bottom with spade. Keep small roots intact.

Slide tarp under rootball. Gather and tie tarp around the base of stems. Move shrub to new site.

Set shrub in hole, remove tarp. Backfill with soil to previous level; water; apply 2 inches of mulch.

A Guide to Shrubs

SPRING

You can depend on these spring-flowering shrubs to provide a dramatic beginning to the growing season. Read labels carefully to get the exact color and size you want.

AZALEA
Rhododendron spp. and hybrids
4-10 feet tall
Zones 4-8
Wide range of colors; deciduous or evergreen leaves; moist, acid soil; light shade.

FORSYTHIA
Forsythia spp.
6-8 feet tall
Zones 5-9
Yellow flowers; deciduous green leaves that turn red-purple in fall; average to moist, well-drained soil; sun.

SUMMER AND FALL

For a spectacular late-season display, select shrubs with summer or fall flowers or showy fall leaves. Those with beautiful berries will extend the show into winter.

BURNING BUSH
Euonymus alata
10-15 feet tall
Zones 3-9
Inconspicuous flowers in spring; deciduous, dark green leaves turn bright red in fall; average soil; sun/light shade.

BUTTERFLY BUSH
Buddleia davidii
6-8 feet tall
Zones 5-10
Purple, pink, or white flowers in summer; narrow, green, deciduous leaves; moist, well-drained soil; sun.

EVERGREEN

Evergreen shrubs provide year-round interest, making them a good choice for hedges and screens. Their deep green color is an excellent backdrop for flowers.

BOXWOOD
Buxus spp.
6-15 feet tall
Zones 6-10
Small, glossy, dark green leaves on densely branched stems; moist, well-drained soil; sun/light shade.

CHINESE PHOTINIA
Photinia serrulata
20-25 feet tall
Zones 7-10
White spring flowers; bronze-red leaves turn dark green as they age; average soil; sun/light shade.

Planting Bare-Root Shrubs

Mail-order, bare-root stock is sometimes the least expensive to plant. If you order from catalogs in winter, for arrival in early spring, you will be planting your bare-root shrubs while they are still dormant. As soon as possible, unwrap and soak roots a few hours. Planting immediately will give them a chance to develop strong roots before warm weather promotes new top growth. 🌺

1

Inspect bare-root shrubs carefully when you unpack them. Prune off any circling, broken, diseased, or dead roots. Before planting, soak the remaining roots in a bucket of water for several hours or overnight.

LILAC
Syringa spp.
15-20 feet tall
Zones 3-8
Fragrant lavender-purple, pink, or white flowers; deciduous green leaves; average soil; sun/light shade.

MOUNTAIN LAUREL
Kalmia latifolia
15-20 feet tall
Zones 4-7
White or pink flowers mid- to late spring; glossy evergreen leaves; moist but well-drained, acid soil essential; sun/partial shade.

VIBURNUM
Viburnum spp.
6-10 feet tall
Zones 4-9
White flowers, often followed by red or black fruits; deciduous or evergreen leaves; average soil; sun/light shade.

ROCKSPRAY COTONEASTER
Cotoneaster horizontalis
2-3 feet tall
Zones 4-9
Pinkish white spring flowers followed by showy red berries; deciduous, glossy green leaves; average soil; sun.

HYDRANGEA
Hydrangea spp.
10-15 feet tall
Zones 5-8
White, pink, or blue flowers in summer into fall; deciduous green leaves; moist, well-drained soil; light shade.

ROSE-OF-SHARON
Hibiscus syriacus
6-10 feet tall
Zone 6-9
White, pink, or purplish flowers in late summer to fall; deciduous green leaves; average to moist, well-drained soil; sun.

HEAVENLY BAMBOO
Nandina domestica
6-10 feet tall
Zones 6-10
White summer flowers followed by red fruit; glossy green, many-parted leaves; moist, well-drained soil; sun/shade.

JUNIPER
Juniperus spp.
1-10 feet tall
Zones 3-8
Green to silvery blue foliage is needle-like when young and scale-like when mature; average soil; sun/light shade.

YEW
Taxus spp.
6-40 feet tall
Zone 5-8
Tiny flowers in early summer may be followed by red fruits; needle-like green foliage; average soil; sun/light shade. Poisonous seeds.

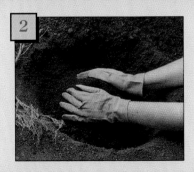

2 — Prepare the planting area by digging a hole large enough to hold the shrub's roots without bending them. Make a cone of soil in the center of the hole. Set the center of the plant on top of the cone.

3 — Spread the roots out as evenly as possible over the cone. Adjust the height of cone if needed, so that crown is even with surrounding soil. Fill in around roots with soil. Water thoroughly, then mulch.

Roses

HYBRID TEA AND OTHERS

Roses have long been considered the ultimate symbol of romance and beauty. Among them, the hybrid tea, which comes in a dazzling array of colors and blooms all season long on elegant stems, continues to be the favorite. It's easy to understand when you see the soft shading of 'Peace' or experience the classic form, dark-red color, and strong scent of 'Chrysler Imperial'.

Of course, hybrid teas aren't the only roses you can grow in your garden. Polyanthas such as 'The Fairy'—compact plants with clusters of flowers throughout the season—are lovely in small landscapes. Floribundas—created from hybrid teas and polyanthas—are most effective planted in groups of the same kind for a mass of color. Grandifloras, typically used as cutting roses, are the tall queens of the garden, with enormous, abundant blooms on long stems. Most old garden roses are extremely hardy, as are modern shrub roses. Miniature roses resemble their larger relatives but often are hardier than hybrid teas and are especially striking placed in front of other plants.

Whichever roses you choose to own, give them full sun, fertile soil, space, and good drainage to ensure success. 🌸

SHRUB ROSES

Shrub roses not only have beautiful blooms but fuller, sturdier forms than other roses. They tend to be more tolerant than hybrid teas of their growing conditions, and many, such as 'Elmshorn' with its clusters of pink blooms, do well mixed with perennials and vines to create a romantic, cottage-garden look. They can be used for colorful, informal hedges or planted in front of evergreens as highlights. A row of shrub roses often makes an attractive and quite effective barrier planting.

When choosing a shrub rose, you'll want to consider that most species and antique shrub roses (gallicas, damasks, albas, centifolias) produce one spectacular show of blossoms each season, while most modern shrub roses (hybrid rugosas, English roses, hybrid musks, polyanthas) are repeat bloomers.

Shrub roses will grow well if given full sun and fertile, well-drained soil. In fact, many of them are easier to grow than other kinds of roses, since shrub roses are often more resistant to black spot, rust, and other common rose diseases. Shrub roses also tend to need less pruning to produce a good display of flowers—a plus if pruning isn't one of your favorite gardening activities. ✿

Selecting Healthy Roses

Research roses to consider in books, magazines, catalogs, nurseries, botanical gardens, and by asking gardening friends and neighbors.

If possible, slide container roses out of their pots and inspect the roots. They should be visible but not circling or heavily matted.

A beautiful rose garden begins with healthy plants. Carefully selecting your roses when you shop will help reduce disease problems after planting, reduce maintenance chores, and give you more time to enjoy the fabulous flowers.

Spring is generally a good time to shop for roses at nurseries and garden centers. Bare-root roses (those sold in bags or boxes, with no soil around the roots) are sold while they are still dormant, so look for them in the early spring. Container roses are usually available throughout the growing season, although you'll find the best selection in the spring. If you buy your roses from a mail-order company, you can shop any time. The company will send your roses at the appropriate planting time for your particular area.

Whether you buy locally or through a catalog, make sure you choose a reputable supplier. Many older cultivars are available only through mail order from specialist nurseries, so if you plan to buy this way, check with gardening friends and neighbors about their experiences with different companies. Or start by ordering one or two plants, then judge their quality for yourself before placing a larger order. Regardless of where you shop, look for roses that are described as disease-resistant, either on the label or in the catalog description. By choosing roses that are naturally less prone to black spot (a fungal leaf spot), powdery mildew, and other common rose diseases, you will greatly reduce the chance of problems after planting.

Bare-root roses should be dormant when you buy them and should be planted before leaves emerge from the buds. Reject plants that have already started producing new growth. Check their stems carefully, too; they should be plump and vigorous. Wrinkled stems are a sign that the plant has dried out in the past, and it probably will not adapt well after planting.

Healthy container-grown roses have unblemished foliage that is usually a rich medium-to-dark-green color, sometimes with a reddish tinge (especially on new growth). Avoid buying plants with yellowing, dusty gray patches, or black spots; these are common signs of disease problems. When you check for signs of pest problems, make sure you inspect the undersides of the leaves; pests often hide there. Do not buy roses with any visible pests or signs of pest or disease damage, even if they are on sale. A sick plant is no bargain at any price, and will put your other garden plants at risk.

Look for container-grown roses that have well-balanced top growth, with at least three or four sturdy stems per plant.

Choose plants with smooth, firm green or red canes. Avoid plants with discolored, shriveled, or spindly stems.

If plant is in bloom, avoid flowers that are shriveled, or those with spotted petals, which may indicate disease.

Pick potted roses with vigorous green or reddish foliage, with no spotting, insect webbing, damage, or discoloration.

HERE'S HOW

PROPERLY SPACING ROSES

If you are planting more than one rose, make sure you consider the mature size of each plant so that you allow enough room between them at planting time. Miniature roses, such as 'Cupcake', need only 1 to 2 feet between plants, while 4 to 6 feet is generally adequate spacing for shrub roses, such as 'Bonica'. For other roses, space plants 2 to 3 feet apart in cool climates and 3 to 4 feet apart if you live in a warmer climate.

These spacings will allow your roses to grow vigorously without crowding each other, reducing your pruning chores. Adequate spacing also will encourage good air circulation around leaves and stems, so wet foliage will dry quickly. This discourages the spread of powdery mildew, black spot, and other rose diseases.

Planting Potted Roses

Potted roses adapt quickly to a new site with minimal care, whether you are introducing them into an existing garden or creating a new bed. In fact, you can plant potted roses any time the ground isn't frozen.

For a new garden, choose a well-drained, sunny site. Loosen the top 1 foot of soil with a spading fork, then work in a 2- to 3-inch layer of compost or some well-rotted manure. An existing bed will also benefit from the addition of the same soil amendments.

HAVE ON HAND:

▶ Gloves

▶ Bucket of water

▶ Spade or shovel

▶ Spading fork

▶ Pruning shears

▶ Mulch

If roses were grown in your planting bed in the past, they may have left diseases in the soil. You might want to opt for a different planting site.

Before soaking your new rose, remove all labels, wires, and plastic loops that can damage stems. Save labels for spacing suggestions and other plant requirements and information. After soaking, you may have to squeeze the pot sides in several places before the rose will slide out. You can also carefully slit the sides of the pot and peel it away from the rootball.

If your rose is grafted, you'll note a slightly swollen area called a graft union near the base of the stem. In Zone 5 or colder regions, mulch your rose heavily in winter, covering the graft union.

Fertilize 4 to 6 weeks after planting with a balanced, organic fertilizer. Water regularly and thoroughly at plant base to encourage root growth and to keep leaves dry and disease resistant. ❧

Soak rootball in water for 1 hour before planting. Dig hole as deep as pot and twice as wide.

Loosen soil at bottom of hole. Slide rose out of pot. Free matted or tangled roots. Prune damaged roots.

Set plant in center of hole with the graft union just above soil level. Fill hole with soil and firm lightly.

Water rose thoroughly to settle soil around roots. Apply 2 inches of mulch, leaving graft union exposed.

Transplanting Roses

Roses can be successfully moved from one part of your garden to another when they are dormant; in fall or early spring. Gardeners in cold winter climates will have greater success in spring when plants are naturally gearing up for a new growing season.

Before digging up the rose you want to move, prepare your new planting site so exposed roots won't dry out before replanting.

When choosing a new place for your rose, avoid spots where other roses have grown within at least 2 years. Roses moved to sites where others have recently grown often develop a mysterious soil-borne malady known as "rose sickness." You can successfully move a single plant into an existing bed by digging a planting hole 18 inches deep and 2 feet wide, and refilling it with soil from another part of the garden. But, if you will be transplanting several roses, you may want to consider an entirely new planting area.

To make transplanting hybrid tea and floribunda roses easier, prune one-third of the canes, or enough to keep the stems and roots in proportion to each other. If you know the rose you are moving is particularly slow growing, prune more lightly. On shrub or climbing roses, carefully tie canes with twine so they won't be in your way or snap off while you are working. If you plant on uneven ground, make a lip of soil around the plant to retain water. 🌺

HAVE ON HAND:

- ▶ Sturdy gloves, protective clothing
- ▶ Spade
- ▶ Spading fork
- ▶ Tarp
- ▶ Pruning shears
- ▶ Water
- ▶ Mulch

Wear protective clothing. Use spading fork to dig planting hole 1 foot wider than rootball, 18 inches deep.

Dig a narrow 18-inch-deep trench around plant, at least 1 foot out from outermost stems on all sides.

Lever rootball out of ground with spading fork. Set on tarp. Trim damaged roots; wrap with tarp to move.

Center rose in new hole at same level as before. Backfill, making soil lip if needed. Water and mulch.

A Guide to Roses

FOR FLOWER BORDERS

Roses are a natural addition to perennial beds, providing height, color, and fragrance to complement other flowers. Plant tall roses at back, shorter roses in middle or front.

HYBRID RUGOSA
Rosa 'Frau Dagmar Hartopp'
To 3 feet tall
Zones 3-8
Silvery pink, single, fragrant flowers late spring through fall; bright red hips. Well-drained soil; sun. Disease resistant.

HYBRID RUGOSA
Rosa 'Hansa'
4-5 feet tall
Zones 3-8
Double, fragrant, purple-red flowers through summer; orange-red hips. Well-drained soil; sun. Disease resistant.

FOR HEDGES AND MASSING

With their thorny stems and striking flowers, roses make effective and attractive hedges. They also look impressive planted in groups of three or five for a mass of color.

FLORIBUNDA
Rosa 'Betty Prior'
3-4 feet tall
Zones 5-9
Single, bright pink, slightly fragrant flowers late spring to fall; well-drained soil; sun. Vigorous; disease resistant.

MODERN SHRUB ROSE
Rosa 'Bonica'
4-5 feet tall
Zones 4-9
Double, light pink flowers mainly in late spring, repeat bloom through fall; well-drained soil; sun. Disease resistant.

FOR WALLS AND FENCES

Make the most of your gardening space by training climbing roses over walls and fences. They are ideal for covering trellises, arbors, and arches with beautiful summer blooms.

CLIMBER
Rosa 'America'
9-12 feet tall
Zones 5-9
Double, strongly scented, salmon pink flowers through summer; well-drained soil; sun. Disease resistant.

CLIMBER
Rosa 'Blaze'
10-12 feet tall
Zones 5-9
Double, slightly fragrant, scarlet flowers mid-season with excellent repeat; well-drained soil; sun. Moderate disease resistance. Very popular.

Planting Bare-Root Roses

Bare-root roses tend to be less expensive than container-grown roses, and they are equally easy to grow. Plant them in the spring in areas with severe winters, late fall to early winter elsewhere. Check for the graft union, a swollen area just above the roots. Set the graft union just above the soil surface when planting. 🌸

1

Prune off damaged roots, then soak the plants in a bucket of water overnight. In the meantime, dig a planting hole 18 inches deep and 24 inches wide.

FLORIBUNDA
Rosa 'Iceberg'
3-4 feet tall
Zones 5-9
Large clusters of double, fragrant, white flowers from late spring through summer. Moderate disease resistance.

HYBRID TEA
Rosa 'Peace'
4-6 feet tall
Zones 5-9
Double, scented, pink-and-yellow flowers in summer. Well-drained soil; sun. Somewhat disease susceptible.

WILD SHRUB ROSE
Rosa glauca 'Red-leaved Rose'
4-5 feet tall
Zones 2-8
Bright pink flowers in early summer; red hips; gray-purple leaves. Well-drained soil; afternoon shade. Disease resistant.

MODERN SHRUB ROSE
Rosa 'Carefree Wonder'
To 5 feet tall
Zones 5-9
Double, deep pink flowers, lighter on reverse; late spring through fall; well-drained soil; sun. Disease resistant.

POLYANTHA
Rosa 'The Fairy'
2-3 feet tall
Zones 4-9
Double, medium-pink flowers from late spring to frost; well-drained soil; sun/light shade. Disease resistant.

HYBRID RUGOSA
Rosa rugosa 'Roseraie de l'Haÿ'
6-9 feet tall
Zones 2-8
Double, deep pink, fragrant flowers late spring and summer; bright red hips; well-drained soil; sun. Very thorny. Disease resistant.

CLIMBER
Rosa 'Climbing Cecile Brunner'
To 20 feet tall
Zones 5-9
Miniature hybrid tea form (called the Buttonhole rose); pink flowers early summer with good repeat; well-drained soil; sun. Vigorous; disease resistant.

KORDESII CLIMBER
Rosa 'Dortmund'
To 10 feet tall
Zones 5-9
Single, lightly fragrant, white-centered red flowers mainly in late spring; red hips; well-drained soil; sun. Disease resistant. Fine pillar rose.

LARGE-FLOWERED CLIMBER
Rosa 'Golden Showers'
To 10 feet tall
Zones 6-9
Large, lightly scented, golden yellow flowers, profuse in late spring and early summer; well-drained soil; sun. Susceptible to black spot.

2 Form a cone of soil in the center of the planting hole. Set the plant on top of the cone. Adjust cone height so the graft union is just above the surface of the soil.

3 Spread roots evenly over the cone. Backfill with soil and water thoroughly. Add a 2-inch layer of mulch; don't cover the graft union.

4. Propagating Techniques

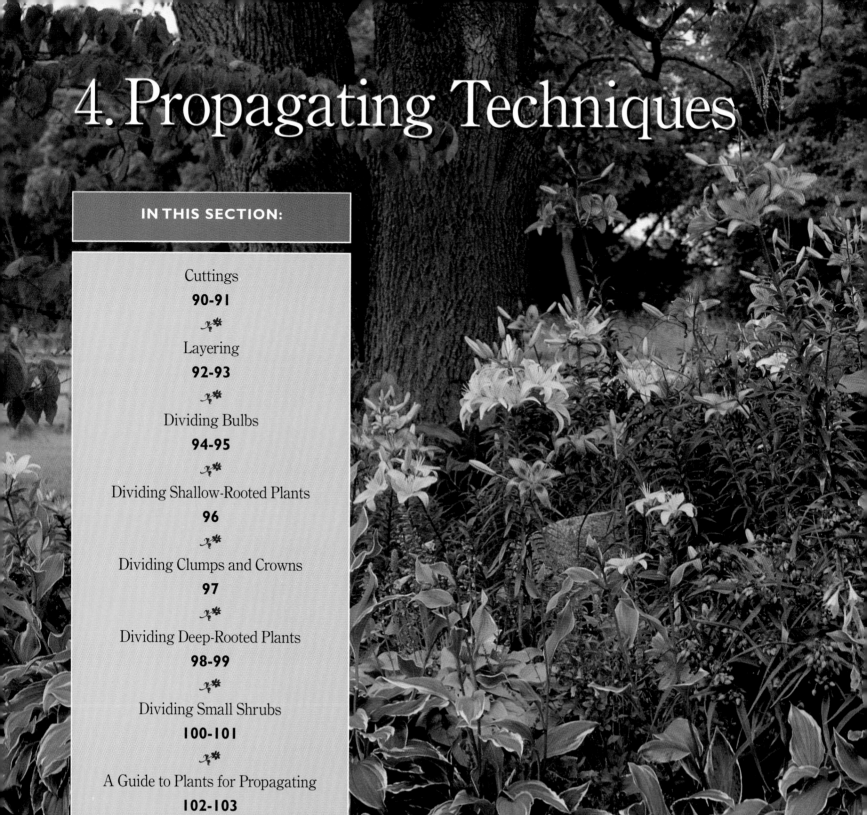

IN THIS SECTION:

I t's inevitable—once you start your first garden, you'll want to plant another, and another. But filling your yard with gorgeous flowers and fabulous foliage can get expensive if you're buying all those new plants. The secret to having all the plants you want without draining your bank account is to learn the tricks of plant propagation.

At the beginning of the previous chapter, you learned how to grow garden plants from seed. That's a great way to start large numbers of plants quickly, but you may have to wait months or years for them to mature and bloom. In addition, the resulting seedlings may vary in height and color, which means you don't always know what you're getting. If you want large plants more quickly, or if you want to be certain you'll get an exact replica of your favorite plant, try "vegetative" propagation. This refers to taking an already-growing part of a plant—usually a piece of shoot or root—and providing the right conditions for it to develop into a whole new plant. You can also divide a large plant into two or more smaller ones, or encourage a shoot to make roots while it is still attached to the original plant.

In this chapter, you'll discover the basics of several easy types of vegetative propagation, including stem and root cuttings, layering, and division. Learn one or more of these easy techniques and your only challenge may be figuring out what to do with all the extra young plants! 🌺

Cuttings

STEM CUTTINGS

Stem cuttings—small sections of vigorous, healthy shoots—will give you exact replicas of your plants in half the time it takes to grow them from seed. For best success, find pest-free shoots without buds or open flowers, and provide humidity so they won't wilt.

A 4-inch pot can hold three to five cuttings spaced so leaves don't touch (to discourage disease). Insert a small stake or pencil into the pot before covering it with a plastic bag, to keep the bag from resting on the cuttings. You won't need to water again until the cuttings have rooted and you've removed the bag.

If you can't plant the rooted cuttings right away, wrap them in a moist paper towel and place in a plastic bag. ✿

HAVE ON HAND:

▶ Pruning shears or garden scissors
▶ 4-inch pot with drainage holes
▶ Moist potting soil
▶ Water
▶ Small stake or pencil
▶ Clear plastic bag
▶ Rubber band

In any season, snip a 3- to 5-inch section from end of healthy shoot, below a leaf and stem juncture (node). Remove leaves from bottom half.

Set bottom half of cutting in potting mix; water. Insert stake or pencil. Cover with plastic bag secured with rubber band. Set in indirect sun.

HERE'S HOW

CARING FOR CUTTINGS

Cuttings will root best in warm conditions (60° to 70°F) with bright but indirect light. Never set plastic-covered cuttings in direct sun—the air in the bag will heat up quickly and "cook" your cuttings. When new growth appears, usually in 3 to 4 weeks, remove the bag. If the cuttings resist a gentle tug, they are rooting and the bag can be left off. If not, replace the bag and check again in a week.

Two or three days after removing the bag permanently, move the cuttings to a sunny spot. Water as needed to keep the potting soil evenly moist. Wait another week or two to transplant rooted cuttings to individual pots. Your new plants are ready for the garden or for a bigger container when they are securely rooted in their pots and are growing vigorously.

ROOT CUTTINGS

Some perennials, such as bleeding heart and Oriental poppy, will produce shoots from sections of root, called root cuttings. Root cuttings generally produce plants identical to the parent. Some variegated plants, however, will have solid green foliage if you grow them from root pieces.

Mark exact location with a stake while plant is in flower but dig in late fall. Choose fleshy roots as thick as a pencil. The root piece closest to the crown will develop shoots, the other end will develop roots. A 4-inch pot will hold three to six root cuttings.

After potting, set cuttings in a cool, protected place. Water only if the soil dries; wet soil can encourage rot. Transplant when top growth appears. ❦

HAVE ON HAND:

▶ Shovel

▶ Water

▶ Sharp, clean knife

▶ 4-inch pot

▶ Moist potting soil

In late fall or winter, use a shovel to dig up the parent plant. Wash off clinging soil so roots can be seen clearly. Choose pencil-thick roots to cut.

Trim chosen roots from plant; keep track of which ends are closest to crown; keep roots moist. Trim parent plant so that roots and top are equal.

Cut these roots into 2-inch sections, making a straight cut at the crown end and a slant cut at the root end for easy identification.

Insert the cuttings into a pot of moist potting soil, with straight-cut ends at the top. Set in a cool place. Replace parent plant in your garden.

Layering

Some plant stems can be encouraged to produce roots while they are still attached to the parent plant. This technique, known as layering, involves bending a plant stem to the ground so roots will form where the stem touches the soil. Layering takes longer than stem cuttings (several months instead of several weeks), but it's a way to propagate shrubs and vines, especially woody plants, that don't root easily from cuttings. Try it with clematis, flowering quince, mountain laurel, azalea and rhododendron, and lilac.

In order to succeed at layering, you'll need a young shoot that is growing close to the ground. (Young shoots take root more readily than older, woody stems, and they are easier to bend.) If your shrub doesn't have a suitable young stem, you may be able to encourage one to develop by cutting a taller stem to within 4 to 6 inches of the ground; do this in the fall. Most gardeners layer only one or two stems at a time on each plant, but if you have enough room and enough suitable shoots, you can layer as many stems per plant as you wish.

Water thoroughly around the shrub or vine the day before layering to make the soil easier to dig. Working a few handfuls of compost into the soil of the layering hole can help promote vigorous rooting. You can also encourage faster root development by dusting the notched part of the stem with rooting hormone, a powder sold in most garden centers.

Water regularly to keep the layered area moist. Some stems will root by the end of the first growing season. If they don't feel securely rooted, check them in the fall and again the following spring. When a layer is well rooted, cut it from the parent plant where the stem enters the ground. Leave the severed layer in place for several months, until the following spring or fall; then transplant it to another part of the garden. ❧

HAVE ON HAND:

- ▶ Trowel or shovel
- ▶ Knife
- ▶ Water
- ▶ Stake
- ▶ String
- ▶ Brick or flat rock

In early spring, select a young, flexible stem near the base of the plant you've chosen to layer. Gently bend the stem to the ground.

Bend stem so the notch is in the hole. Replace soil, leaving stem tip exposed. Water thoroughly. If needed, tie stem tip to a stake to hold upright.

Mark a point on the ground about 1 foot from the tip of the stem. Dig a hole in the soil below point, 4 inches deep and about 6 inches wide.

Cut a shallow notch on the underside of the stem, about 9 inches from the tip. Remove leaves 3 inches on either side of the notch.

Lay a brick or a flat rock over the buried part of the stem to hold the stem down and to help keep the soil moist.

In the fall, remove the brick or rock. Tug lightly at stem base to determine whether it has rooted; a well-rooted stem will feel firmly anchored.

HERE'S HOW

MOUND LAYERING

If you want to get many new plants from a single clump, use a technique called mound layering. It works well with perennials that tend to get woody stems and die out in the center, such as lavender, sage, southernwood, thyme, and wormwood. Simply mound sandy soil over the base of the stems in early spring. A 4- to 5-inch mound is sufficient; make sure at least 1 to 2 inches of each shoot tip is still exposed.

In late summer or fall, gently pull back the mounded soil to check for roots along the stems. If roots aren't visible, replace the soil and check again in spring. When you see roots, cut the rooted shoots from the parent plant. Plant them in pots or in an out-of-the-way nursery bed until they are ready to be transplanted into the garden.

Dividing Bulbs

Division is a quick and easy way to increase your bulb collection. This simple technique allows you to expand plantings of your favorite bulbs without the expense of buying new ones. It's also a great way to add new life to crowded, overgrown clumps of bulbs that are flowering poorly. Pot-grown bulbs normally need dividing every two to three years; those in the ground may only need dividing every three to five years.

The best time to divide hardy bulbs, such as daffodils, crocus, and tulips, is just as they go dormant after flowering. You will want to wait until their foliage is about half yellowed. By that time, the bulbs will have stored plenty of food, but they will still be easy to find. Replant bulbs immediately after you divide them, or store them for later planting (see Lifting and Storing Bulbs, page 41).

Plant stored bulbs as you would newly purchased ones in late summer to early fall. Large bulbs will bloom as usual the next year. Small offsets may take two to three years to flower, but will produce a beautiful display once established. If you wish, you can plant these bulblets in a corner of your vegetable garden or in another out-of-the-way spot; then move them to the flower garden once they reach blooming size.

Tender bulbs generally adapt best to division in early spring, before or just as their new growth is starting. On gladiolus, simply pick off the small cormels before you set the parent corms in the garden. Plant the cormels in a "holding bed" for two to three years (lifting and storing them each winter), until they reach flowering size. Divide dahlias, tuberous begonias, and caladiums by cutting them apart with a sharp, clean knife. In addition, dusting the cut surfaces with powdered sulfur and letting them dry for a day or two before potting them up will help prevent disease.

HARDY. *In summer after foliage yellows, lift bulbs with spading or hand fork, depending on depth. Shake off excess soil to expose bulbs.*

TENDER. *Remove tubers from storage in late winter. Look for small pink buds on the crown, where the roots join the stem.*

HAVE ON HAND:

▶ Spading fork or hand fork

▶ Sharp knife

▶ Trowel or bulb planter

▶ Water

▶ Mulch

▶ Pots and potting soil

Gently break the clump apart with your fingers to separate individual bulbs. Discard any bulbs that are diseased or damaged.

Pull off or cut bulb leaves. Replant bulbs into prepared soil at appropriate depth. Water thoroughly, then top with a 1-inch layer of mulch.

Using a sharp knife, carefully cut each clump in half or into thirds, making sure each division has at least one healthy growth bud.

Plant divisions in potting soil in 6-inch pots. Set in a warm, bright place indoors; water regularly. Plant in garden in mid to late spring.

HERE'S HOW

PROPAGATING LILIES

Lilies are particularly easy to propagate because they produce tiny new bulbs called bulblets and bulbils. Bulblets form along the buried part of the stem; bulbils form where the leaves join the flowering stem above ground. Gather bulbils by picking them from the stems in late summer. Collect bulblets by digging up lily bulbs when the stalk turns yellow; pick off the bulblets and replant the main bulb. Plant bulbils and bulblets in pots and set in a sheltered place outdoors over winter. Plant them in the garden or holding bed the following year; they may take another two to three years to reach flowering size.

Dividing Shallow-Rooted Plants

Shallow-rooted perennials are simple and gratifying to divide, making it easy to fill your garden with your favorite foliage and flowers from only a few starter plants. Use your shallow-rooted spreaders as fillers in new beds and borders, until larger plants become well established. Then, divide the spreaders and plant them as ground cover in other areas. You'll soon have enough for yourself and extras to share.

The best time to divide shallow-rooted plants is when they are in leafy growth. As a general rule, divide spring and early summer-flowering plants such as ajuga and spotted lamium in late summer or fall. Fall bloomers, such as plumbago, adapt better to spring division. It's best to divide during a spell of cool, cloudy weather to prevent excess wilting of already stressed plants. If the ground is dry, water thoroughly the day before dividing. This is also a good time to prepare your new planting site.

Keep in mind that large sections of plants will recover more quickly than small ones. Damaged or dead sections will always be welcome in your compost pile.

After planting, regular, thorough watering is critical to help shallow-rooted plants get reestablished. If the weather is sunny and warm, protect replanted divisions for a week or so with over-turned, slitted boxes or black, polyethylene-mesh shade cloth from a garden center or hardware store. 🌸

HAVE ON HAND:

▶ Spading fork or shovel

▶ Pruning shears

▶ Water

▶ Seaweed extract or fish emulsion

▶ Mulch

Lift shallow-rooted plants from the ground with spading fork or shovel. Shake excess soil from roots.

Cut back top growth on each section by ½ to ⅔. Replant the divisions immediately into prepared soil.

Divide plants into sections, using your hands. Make sure each section has ample healthy roots.

Water thoroughly; feed with seaweed extract or fish emulsion. Keep mulch away from stems.

Dividing Clumps and Crowns

Division is a fast and easy way to multiply many clump- and crown-forming plants such as iris or daisies. An established clump can yield from two to six or more new plants, all identical to the original. This is a great way to turn a single specimen into a bold, showy drift of plants. Division helps keep clumps vigorous, since you can discard the dead inner parts that develop as new outer growth crowds out the center. Most perennials grow best if divided every three to five years.

HAVE ON HAND:

► Spade, shovel, or trowel
► Knife (for tough clumps)
► Hand fork (for loose clumps)
► Water
► Seaweed extract or fish emulsion
► Mulch

As you work in or walk through your garden, you will recognize the plants that look ready for division. They will be the plants that are flowering poorly or not at all, or look too big for the spot they are in. Jot down their names in your gardening notebook so you'll remember which plants to divide when the time is right (fall for early bloomers, spring for others).

To prevent wilt, divide plants during cool, cloudy weather. If it's hot and dry, water thoroughly the day before you plan to divide. Save only the most vigorous-looking sections for replanting; dead or unproductive parts can join the compost pile. A dose of seaweed extract or fish emulsion will give an immediate boost to developing roots. Laying down 2 inches of organic mulch will also promote root growth by keeping roots from drying out. But avoid moist mulch piled against stems, which can lead to rot. 🌿

Dig a circle around plant, 2 to 3 inches from the outermost stems. Lift the rootball; shake off loose soil.

Cut back top growth by ½ to ⅔. Pull or cut clump apart so each section has roots and top growth.

Replant only the healthiest-looking sections in prepared soil. Firm the soil around crowns.

Water deeply. Feed with seaweed extract or fish emulsion for root growth. Mulch away from crowns.

Dividing Deep-Rooted Plants

While most perennials thrive when divided every three to five years, there are a few that grow best when left undisturbed. These include columbines, purple coneflower, lupines, monkshood, Oriental poppies, and peonies. Whenever possible, it's better to start new plants of these perennials from seed. But if a long-established clump is beginning to flower poorly, or if you want to share part of a special plant with a friend, you may need to resort to division. You have a good chance of success if you take extra care.

For best results, choose a spell of cool, cloudy weather in spring or fall so that already stressed plants don't suffer from wilting. Prepare your new planting site first, so that divisions can be replanted immediately. If the weather has been dry, water your plants deeply the day before you plan to divide them.

Check around the base for rooted sideshoots before digging up the whole clump. If you find some, carefully separate them from the parent with a trowel or spade, then move them to the new location. Where no offsets are visible, you'll need to dig up the whole plant and separate at the crowns, the portion of the plant where root meets stem.

Remember that larger sections of plant will tend to reestablish more quickly. Smaller, or weak-looking parts, along with some inevitable broken roots and stems, can be set aside for compost.

Regular watering after replanting is vital in order to help divided plants produce new roots. A dose of seaweed extract or fish emulsion (follow application instructions on the package) will encourage quick root growth. Adding a layer of organic mulch will help keep the soil evenly moist. If the weather is warm and sunny, shade your new divisions for a week or so after planting with tented newspaper weighted around the edges or overturned, slitted boxes or black, polyethylene-mesh shade cloth. ❧

HAVE ON HAND:

► Spade

► Spading fork

► Water

► Knife

► Seaweed extract or fish emulsion

► Mulch

Cut a deep circle around plant with a spade, 3 to 4 inches out from the outermost stems so that damage to roots is minimal.

Carefully separate tightly packed crowns with a sharp knife. Make sure each piece has both roots and either buds or top growth.

Lift the clump with care by inserting a spading fork deeply in order to get as much of the root system as possible without damage.

Wash off soil so that you can see the roots you're working with. If possible, separate the roots with your fingers.

Replant sections immediately into prepared soil to the crown level. Firm soil around the crown by tamping with foot, and water thoroughly.

Feed with seaweed extract or fish emulsion to encourage root growth. Apply a 2-inch layer of mulch. To prevent rot, do not cover the crown.

HERE'S HOW

WHEN TO DIVIDE

The best time to divide most spring-and early summer-flowering plants is in late summer.

Midsummer is better for Oriental poppies and bearded iris.

Spring is an optimum time for other summer- and fall-flowering plants.

If you can't divide a particular plant during the ideal season, you can still get good results at other times. Cut leafy growth back by ½ to ⅔ before replanting to reduce water loss. Then proceed with division as described.

Dividing Small Shrubs

SUCKERING SHRUBS

Small shrubs are invaluable for adding height and seasonal color to the garden. Those with shallow roots are particularly useful as screens and hedges, since they tend to send out "suckers" or new shoots from their roots, which spread to produce a dense barrier. You can help them fill in more quickly by digging up rooted suckers in spring or fall and transplanting them to empty spots. You can also move these divisions into your flowering beds and borders for additional color.

This technique works well with many common shrubs, including barberries, deutzias, shrubby dogwoods, Japanese kerria, nongrafted lilacs, mock oranges, and spireas. Be aware that suckers from the bases of grafted plants, such as many lilac cultivars and hybrid roses, will not resemble the top growth of the parent plant; they will instead look like the plant that was used for the root system.

With regular watering and mulching, divisions with sturdy root systems will reestablish themselves fairly quickly after replanting. If a division has only a few fibrous roots, however, it will need your special attention. Instead of transplanting directly into its permanent location in the garden, plant it first in a container of potting soil, set it in a shady spot for a few weeks, and water it regularly to keep the soil moist and encouraging to the formation of new roots. After one or two seasons, when the division is established and growing vigorously, transplant it to the desired location. ❧

HAVE ON HAND:

▶ Spading fork

▶ Pruning shears

▶ Water

▶ Mulch

When plant is dormant, loosen soil around sucker with spading fork. Ensure it has fibrous roots at base.

Cut underground link between sucker and parent; lift from soil. Replace soil around parent plant.

Trim new division's main root to where fibrous roots branch out. Replant into prepared soil.

Firm soil around the crown. Water thoroughly. Apply a 2-inch layer of mulch; do not cover the crown.

CLUMPING SHRUBS

Divide your clumping shrubs to create mass ornamental plantings that will produce a striking effect. They are a bit more work to divide, since you'll need to dig up the entire plant, but your result will be several useful divisions of the same size. Division is also a smart way to extend your plant-buying budget. You can, for instance, buy and plant one shrub in your garden and multiply your collection by division in a few short years.

Division works best when plants are dormant, in early spring or in fall. If the weather has been dry, soak the ground around the shrub the day before you plan to divide.

Make sure the shrub you want to propagate has multiple stems and plentiful roots at ground level before you dig it up. Ideally, there should be at least 1 inch between the stems. Tightly packed woody stems are difficult to divide without injuring the plant.

After replanting, prune out any damaged stems, and water deeply. Maintain a thorough and regular watering schedule to help the plant re-establish its deep root system. A 2-inch layer of organic mulch will help to keep the soil evenly moist; but keep mulch away from stems to prevent their rotting. A dose of seaweed extract after planting will help promote quick rooting since its liquid form is easily absorbed by hungry roots. ❦

HAVE ON HAND:

▶ Spade or shovel

▶ Spading fork

▶ Ax (for tough clumps)

▶ Pruning shears or loppers

▶ Water

▶ Mulch

Dig a trench about 1 foot out from the outermost stems. Loosen soil around roots with a spading fork.

Lift the rootball from the hole, and shake off loose soil so you can clearly see where stem meets root.

Separate into sections, each with root and top growth. Pull apart with hands, or cut with spade or ax.

Replant sections into prepared soil. Water thoroughly and mulch; keep mulch away from stems.

A Guide to Plants for Propagating

ANNUALS

Sowing seed is the most common propagation technique for annuals. Stem cuttings is another. Keep your favorites from year to year with either method.

COLEUS
Coleus x hybridus
6-24 inches tall
All zones
Wide range of leaf color and pattern; average to moist, well-drained soil; partial shade. Sow spring; stem cuttings any time.

GERANIUM
Pelargonium x hortorum
1-2 feet tall
All zones
Red, pink, salmon, white flowers; average soil; sun/part shade. Sow late winter; take stem cuttings any time.

PERENNIALS

Buying perennials to fill a garden can be pricey. Many are easy to propagate by division or stem cuttings. In a few years, you'll fill your garden with long-lasting plants.

AJUGA
Ajuga reptans
4-8 inches tall
Zones 3-9
Spikes of blue flowers in spring; average to moist, well-drained soil; sun/light shade. Dig rooted plantlets in growing season.

ASTER
Aster spp.
3-6 feet tall
Zones 3-8
Blue, purple, pink, white flowers; moist, well-drained soil; sun/light shade. Divide early spring; stem cuttings late spring.

BULBS

The fastest and easiest way to expand your bulb display is to divide the clumps every three to five years, normally after their foliage has begun to turn yellow.

CROCUS
Crocus spp. and hybrids
3-4 inches tall
Zones 3-8
Purple, pink, yellow, or white flowers; average soil; sun/partial shade. Divide both spring- and fall-flowering kinds in early summer.

DAFFODIL
Narcissus spp. and hybrids
6-20 inches tall
Zones 4-8
Yellow or white blooms, often with center cup or trumpet; average soil; sun/partial shade. Divide in early to midsummer.

Creating a Nursery Bed

A nursery bed is a special spot set aside for young plants to grow to garden size. It is invaluable if you enjoy propagating your own plants. Since the seedlings, cuttings, and divisions are all in one place, it's easy to give them the special attention they need, and they won't have to compete with bigger, established garden plants for light, water, and nutrients. 🌺

1

Choose a sunny spot with well-drained soil, preferably in an existing, out-of-the-way bed. Begin with 3 square feet and expand as needed. If the soil isn't already prepared, dig and amend the site as you would for a new garden bed.

IMPATIENS
Impatiens wallerana
6-24 inches tall
All zones
Red, pink, orange, lavender, or white blooms; average to moist soil; part shade. Sow seed in spring; take stem cuttings any time.

WAX BEGONIA
Begonia semperflorens-cultorum hybrids
6-8 inches tall
All zones
Red, pink, white flowers; moist, well-drained soil; part shade. Sow late winter; stem cuttings any time.

VERBENA
Verbena x hybrida
8-12 inches tall
All zones
Flowers in a range of colors; average soil; full sun. Sow seed in late winter; take stem cuttings any time.

CHRYSANTHEMUM
Chrysanthemum x morifolium
1-3 feet tall
Zones 3-9
Flowers in many colors; average soil; sun/light shade. Divide in spring; stem cuttings late spring or early summer.

DAYLILY
Hemerocallis hybrids
1-5 feet tall
Zones 3-9
Flowers in a range of colors; average to moist soil; sun/light shade. Divide clump in spring or fall.

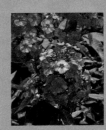

BORDER PHLOX
Phlox spp.
3-4 feet tall
Zones 3-8
Red, pink, purple, or white blooms; moist, well-drained soil; sun/light shade. Divide in spring; stem cuttings early summer, root cuttings in fall.

GLADIOLUS
Gladiolus x hortulanus
2-5 feet tall
All zones
Summer flowers in a range of colors; average soil, sun. Separate small corms from base, plant both in spring. Lift in autumn in cold climates.

LILY
Lilium spp. and hybrids
2-5 feet tall
Zones 4-8
Red, pink, orange, yellow, or white flowers; average soil; sun/part shade. Remove small bulblets to plant in fall.

GRAPE HYACINTH
Muscari spp.
6-8 inches tall
Zones 4-8
Clusters of purple-blue or white flowers; average soil; sun/part shade. Divide in early summer, as leaves die back.

As perennial seedlings and cuttings outgrow their pots, transplant them into the nursery bed. Use also for small bulb, perennial, and shrub divisions until large enough for a bed or border. Plant in rows or blocks; allow 4 inches between plants.

After well-developed plants have been moved to their permanent locations, work a handful or two of compost into each empty spot. Replace with other young plants as they are ready for your nursery bed.

5. Pruning

Pruning is your opportunity to direct the growth of your plants, control their size, and improve their appearance. Proper pruning also has many other benefits, such as improving flower and fruit production, maintaining plant health, and promoting vigorous new growth.

Basically, pruning is cutting. The key to successful pruning is knowing what results to expect, depending on where you make each cut. Cutting just above a bud, called a heading cut, will encourage the buds below the cut to grow. Cutting back to another stem, or to the ground, is called a thinning cut. You'll use thinning cuts to loosen crowded growth, remove suckers and crossing branches, and open the center of a plant to light and air. Thinning cuts are also useful for removing older stems (usually dark brown or gray), to make room for strong new stems (greenish or light brown). Encouraging new growth each year will help plants retain their vigor and bloom generously. And thinning out dead, diseased, or damaged growth will improve plant health and appearance.

Spread your pruning projects through the year to give your plants the individual attention they need. They'll respond with healthy, great-looking growth.

Pruning Flowering Shrubs

SPRING-FLOWERING

Few sights are more welcome to a winter-weary gardener than the brightly colored blooms of spring-flowering shrubs. Treating these early bloomers to a light yearly pruning will keep them looking their best.

Pruning dead or diseased wood back to healthy growth or to the ground improves appearance and allows your shrub to keep its natural form and remain healthy. Be aware, however, that some dead and diseased growth won't be obvious until your shrub has leafed out, so plan for a second pruning a bit later in the season. Of course, you can remove misplaced or weak stems any time. Thinning out crowded, twiggy growth in the center of your shrub will encourage production of vigorous new flowering shoots.

Shrubs that bloom in spring and early summer flower on stems that were produced during the previous growing season or on short sideshoots from those stems. These shrubs need pruning after they flower. Many common garden shrubs fall into this category, including azaleas, flowering quince, deutzias, forsythias, big-leaved hydrangea, Japanese kerria, mock oranges, firethorns, lilacs, viburnums, and old-fashioned weigela.

Avoid the temptation to shear stems uniformly with hedge clippers. Most flowering shrubs respond better to hand-pruning, and retain their natural beauty as well. 🌿

HAVE ON HAND:

► Pruning shears (stems up to ¾-inch diameter)

► Loppers (stems up to 1 ¾-inch diameter)

► Pruning saw (stems over 1 ¾-inch diameter)

After flowering, prune dead, damaged, or diseased stems back to a bud, another stem, or the ground.

Remove up to ⅓ of the oldest stems at the shrub base to stimulate new growth.

Thin crowded growth to base, and spent flower clusters to next strong buds, at a 45° angle away from bud.

Cut back overly long shoots to match other stems, and to give the shrub a well-balanced shape.

LATE-BLOOMING

Summer- and fall-flowering shrubs are valuable additions to any garden, providing height and color to complement low growing perennials and annuals. Examples of these late bloomers include abelias, orange-eye butterfly bush, shrubby crape myrtles, heavenly bamboo, hibiscus, and most hydrangeas.

Unlike spring-flowering shrubs, late-blooming shrubs usually flower on the current season's growth. A yearly pruning in late winter or early spring will promote vigorous new growth, ensuring a super flower display later in the season. Always remove dead or diseased wood first in order to see what you're left with to prune. On newly planted shrubs, trim the main stems back by about a third to produce a strong framework. On established plants, cut out up to half of the oldest stems each year. Cut the remaining stems of orange-eye butterfly bush and shrub-form crape myrtles back to 1 to 2 feet.

Some shrubs are grown more for their colorful stems than for their leaves or flowers. Many shrubby dogwoods, for instance, produce bright red or yellow stems that add a spark of color to winter gardens. On young plants, cut out a third of the oldest stems at the base in spring to promote colorful new growth. Established, vigorous plants grown for their colorful winter stems can withstand hard pruning; to 2 to 3 inches from the base each spring. 🌸

HAVE ON HAND:

▶ Pruning shears (stems up to ¾-inch diameter)

▶ Loppers (stems up to 1¾-inch diameter)

▶ Pruning saw (stems over 1¾-inch diameter)

Prune dead, diseased, damaged stems to the ground, other stem, or above healthy bud to spur growth.

With loppers or saw, cut out up to ½ of oldest stems at the base to make room for new growth.

Thin crowded, twiggy, or poorly placed growth. If two branches rub against each other, remove one.

Prune over-long stems to create a balanced framework. On very vigorous shrubs, cut stems to 8 inches.

Pruning Evergreen Shrubs

Evergreen shrubs form the backbone of the garden, with their handsome forms and soothing green foliage. Many don't need much pruning, but a few well-placed snips at the right time will keep them in peak condition.

Needle-leaved evergreens include such traditional favorites as arborvitae, junipers, and yews. Most can't tolerate heavy pruning, so it's important to trim young plants lightly during their active growing season, when cuts heal faster, to develop the desired shape. Yews are one exception. Reclaim overgrown plants by cutting them back to a 1- to 2-foot framework of branches in spring.

When pruning too-long shoots on established needle-leaved evergreens, reach back into leafy growth to hide your pruning cuts. Don't shear them unless you are willing to do it frequently during the growing season to maintain their formal appearance.

Pruned in late spring, broad-leaved evergreens, including aucuba, boxwoods, camellias, euonymus, and mountain laurel, will reward you all year long. Boxwoods, like yew, will tolerate severe pruning. Rejuvenate your overgrown boxwood by cutting back to a 1- to 2-foot framework of stems in the spring. Consider waiting until November or December to prune shrubs such as hollies, aucuba, mahonia, and euonymus, then use the pruned branches for holiday decor. 🌺

HAVE ON HAND:

▶ Pruning shears (stems up to ¾-inch diameter)

▶ Loppers (stems up to 1¾-inch diameter)

▶ Pruning saw (stems over 1¾-inch diameter)

NEEDLE-LEAVED. *Pinch tips on arborvitae and yews after new growth has hardened off to limit size.*

In early to midsummer, remove any dead tips. Cut longest shoots back to maintain shrub's shape.

BROAD-LEAVED. *In late spring, prune dead, damaged growth. If stems cross, remove one.*

Trim overly long and poorly placed shoots to shape the plant, cutting back to a bud or another stem.

Pruning Vines

If you're nervous about pruning, vines are the right plants to practice on. These tough, vigorous plants can take a hard pruning and come back for more.

Clinging vines, such as Boston ivy and Virginia creeper, often need little more than a bit of thinning to open up crowded growth and remove dead or diseased stems. Since clinging stems won't reattach if they come off their support, it's best to trim loose stem tips back to where they cling.

Other vines need different approaches, depending on flowering time. Vines that flower on new growth, such as hops, passionflowers, and porcelain vine, need heavy pruning in late winter or early spring. Vines that bloom on the previous year's stems, such as honeysuckles, are pruned within a month after flowering ends, so next year's buds have time to form. Trim long shoots back to another stem or to the ground to control size and shape.

Clematis vary in their requirements. Those that bloom once in spring or early summer need pruning just after flowering, to allow next year's flower buds to form on new growth. Prune summer- and fall-bloomers in early spring for strong new stems and blooms. On reblooming clematis, trim shoot tips back to the topmost pair of strong buds in early spring. Or, for one showy display later in the season, cut all of the stems back to the lowest buds. 🌸

HAVE ON HAND:

▶ Pruning shears (stems up to ¾-inch diameter)

▶ Loppers (stems up to 1¾-inch diameter)

▶ Pruning saw (stems over 1¾-inch diameter)

WISTERIA. *In early spring, remove any dead stems. Cut back remaining sideshoots to 2 or 3 buds.*

After bloom, cut off spent flowers. Trim overly long shoots to keep them in balance with rest of plant.

CLEMATIS. *In early spring, cut back summer- and fall-bloomers to lowest pair of strong buds on stem.*

Prune spring-blooming clematis after flowering. Trim new sideshoots back to 2 or 3 pairs of buds.

Pruning Roses

HYBRID TEA

Rose pruning doesn't have to be difficult or complicated. All you need are the right tools and a little knowledge about your particular plants. Pruning your roses will stimulate new growth and result in healthy, vigorous, and attractive plants.

Prune roses when they are dormant (after their leaves drop in fall and before new growth starts in spring), but not when they are frozen. In mild-winter zones you can accomplish most of the necessary pruning in fall and snip out any frost-damaged shoot tips in spring. In cold-winter regions, cut back hybrid tea roses by about half in fall and leave the detailed pruning until late winter or early spring. In this way, buds near the cuts won't be damaged by below-freezing temperatures. Chances are you will only have to prune lightly again in the spring. At worst, you may lose a few stems.

Hybrid tea roses bloom on new wood, so they need moderate to heavy dormant pruning in order to produce a strong framework of main flowering shoots. Keep an eye on your roses during the growing season, pruning out weak, nonflowering stems as necessary. When you cut blooms for the house, cut to a five-leaflet leaf to encourage a second flush. Newly planted roses require food-producing leaves, so when you take flowers take as little of the foliage as possible. ❧

HAVE ON HAND:

▶ Pruning shears (stems up to ¾-inch diameter)
▶ Loppers (stems up to 1 ¾-inch diameter)
▶ Pruning saw (stems over 1 ¾-inch diameter)
▶ Sturdy, thornproof gloves
▶ Wood glue

During dormancy, prune out dead, dying, or diseased shoots. If two stems cross, prune out one.

Thin crowded growth. Make 45° angle cuts, ¼ inch above and away from outward-facing bud.

Prune main stems to 18 inches for small, abundant flowers, or to 1 foot for large, long-stemmed flowers.

Seal all cuts with wood glue to prevent destructive cane borers from entering stems.

SHRUB ROSES AND OTHERS

Different kinds of roses require different pruning approaches. Shrub roses generally need little pruning, but each year you will want to remove diseased or dead wood and cut out a few of the oldest stems at the base. Also, you will want to shorten the longest canes to shape the plant and create a balanced framework of flowering stems. It's important to remove "suckers," shoots from the root of your grafted rose. If allowed to grow, suckers will eventu-

ally kill the flower-producing grafted stock. Snap—don't cut—them off at the base, as cutting can leave buds that will resprout.

Climbing roses generally don't need pruning for the first two years after planting. After that, prune them in the spring. Trim sideshoots to 3 to 6 inches, leaving three or four buds on each. On established plants, cut out one or two of the oldest stems each year.

Floribundas (the term for cluster-flowered roses) form bushy plants that flower best with light pruning, as shown.

To encourage upright growth on a spreading rose, prune to a bud that faces upward, not outward.

Thinning out dense, twiggy growth on any rose will allow for good air circulation around stems and leaves. This enables foliage to dry quickly after rainfall or watering, thereby reducing the risk of the spread of waterborne disease. ❧

HAVE ON HAND:

- ▶ Pruning shears (stems up to ¾-inch diameter)
- ▶ Loppers (stems up to 1 ¾-inch diameter)
- ▶ Pruning saw (stems over 1 ¾-inch diameter)
- ▶ Sturdy, thornproof gloves
- ▶ Wood glue

SHRUB. *During dormancy, remove dead, diseased, or awkward stems. Prune at base, above graft union.*

Thin crowded, twiggy growth. Make 45° angle cuts, ¼ inch above and away from outward-facing bud.

CLIMBING. *Select 6 to 8 best canes; prune out others. Cut main shoots to 2 feet above the ground.*

Reduce sideshoots by ⅓ to ⅔. Seal all cuts with wood glue to prevent cane borers from entering plant.

A Guide to Pruning

LATE WINTER

Important for shrubs that bloom on current season's growth or produce colorful young stems. Also a good time to thin out crowded stems on deciduous shrubs.

BARBERRY
Berberis spp.
6-8 feet tall
Zones 4-10
Deciduous, semi-evergreen, or evergreen leaves; moist, well-drained soil; sun/part shade. Cut a few shoots to ground each year.

BUTTERFLY BUSH
Buddleia davidii
6-8 feet tall
Zones 5-10
Pink, purple, or white summer flowers; deciduous; moist, well-drained soil; sun. Prune to 8-18 inch framework of stems each year.

LATE SPRING

Late spring is a good time to trim evergreen shrubs for shape and to eliminate any winter damage. But prune berry-producing evergreens in late winter.

BOXWOOD
Buxus spp.
6-15 feet tall
Zones 6-10
Glossy, oval, evergreen leaves, slender branches; moist, well-drained soil; sun/light shade. Prune damaged tips; trim to shape.

COTONEASTER
Cotoneaster spp.
3-4 feet tall
Zones 4-9
Pinkish spring flowers; red fall berries; evergreen or deciduous; average soil; sun. Remove dead, damaged, and poorly placed stems yearly.

AFTER FLOWERING

Prune spring and early summer flowering shrubs within a month after their flowers fade. If you wait any later, you'll run the risk of pruning off next year's developing flower buds.

AZALEA
Rhododendron spp.
4-10 feet tall
Zones 4-8
Spring or summer blooms in range of colors; deciduous or evergreen leaves; moist, acid soil; light shade. Cut poorly placed branches.

DEUTZIA
Deutzia spp.
4-6 feet tall
Zones 4-9
White spring flowers on arching stems; deciduous; moist, well-drained soil; sun. Cut up to ⅓ of oldest stems to ground each year.

Pruning Hedges

Pruning hedges doesn't have to be a hassle if you keep a few things in mind. Informal hedges need minimal yearly pruning to stay healthy. Formal hedges require more frequent trimming to look their best. Trim stems at a neat 45° angle, which leaves a small stub that will dry out fast. If you neglect your hedges, don't despair; you may be able to reclaim them with heavy pruning (see Pruning Evergreen Shrubs, page 108).

Formal hedges need several shearings during the season. Trim as needed until midsummer; later pruning promotes tender growth prone to cold damage. Shape the hedge with top slightly narrower than bottom so sun can reach lower growth.

HYDRANGEA
Hydrangea spp.
10-15 feet tall
Zones 5-8
Spring or summer flower clusters; deciduous; moist, well-drained soil; light shade. Remove ⅓ of oldest stems each year.

PRIVET
Ligustrum spp.
10-12 feet tall
Zones 5-9
Many-branched stems with deciduous or evergreen leaves; moist, well-drained soil; sun/light shade. Trim or shear as needed to shape.

RED-TWIG DOGWOOD
Cornus alba, C. sericea
6-8 feet tall
Zones 3-7
Insignificant small white flowers, spring; deciduous leaves; red young stems; moist, well-drained soil; sun/shade. Cut ⅓ of oldest stems each year.

HOLLY
Ilex spp.
8-60 feet tall
Zones 5-8
Evergreen or deciduous shrubs with red or black fall berries; moist, well-drained soil; sun/light shade. Prune only to shape.

JUNIPER
Juniperus spp.
1-10 feet tall
Zones 3-8
Spreading or upright evergreens with needle- or scale-like foliage; average soil; sun/light shade. Trim to shape.

YEW
Taxus spp.
6-40 feet tall
Zones 5-8
Evergreen, needle-like leaves on upright or spreading stems; average soil; sun/light shade. Trim as needed to shape.

FORSYTHIA
Forsythia spp.
6-8 feet tall
Zones 5-9
Bright yellow blooms in early spring; deciduous; average to moist, well-drained soil; sun. Prune ⅓ of oldest stems to ground each year.

LILAC
Syringa spp.
15-20 feet tall
Zones 3-8
Purple, pink, or white spring flowers; deciduous; average soil; sun/light shade. Cut a few of oldest stems at base yearly.

VIBURNUM
Viburnum spp.
6-10 feet tall
Zones 4-9
White flowers in spring; deciduous or evergreen; average soil; sun/light shade. Cut out ⅓ of oldest stems each year.

Prune informal hedges as if plants grew separately, at proper time for the type of plant. Shorten overly long stems to develop a balanced overall shape. Cut individual stems with hand pruners to maintain their natural, layered appearance.

On hedges with variegated leaves, look for nonvariegated branches and prune when they are small by cutting to the first branch below the nonvariegated part. If left to grow, they will outgrow the variegated part of the hedge.

6. Maintaining Your Garden

As your garden grows and thrives, there are a variety of techniques you can use to keep it looking its best. You don't have to be tied down to garden maintenance every summer weekend if you do a little bit each time you're outside. Keep a bucket and pruning shears handy, so you can take them each time you walk around the garden. Make a habit of pinching off dead flowers and pulling out seedling weeds as you see them, and you won't have to set aside whole hours for deadheading or weeding later on. You can also set up stakes and other plant supports early in the season to save emergency staking later on.

When rainfall is lacking, recharge your soil's water reserves with the most efficient and effective irrigation technique for each planting area. You'll also need to apply fertilizers to replace the nutrients used up by your plants as they grow. To minimize watering chores and add some nutrients at the same time, cover the ground between plants with chopped leaves, shredded bark, or other organic mulch.

Don't give up on your garden when the chrysanthemums and other late bloomers signal the approach of cold weather. Fall is the ideal season for many garden projects, including digging new beds, planting, and transplanting. It's also the time to clean up tired, frost-nipped plantings, so they'll be in top shape for spring's return. If you live in a cold climate, you'll also want to take steps to protect your plantings from cold temperatures, drying winds, and hungry animal pests.

This section covers all the basics of caring for your garden throughout the year, so you'll have the pleasure of seeing your ideas—and your plants—grow into a garden you'll enjoy and enjoy showing to others. ❧

Deadheading

Deadheading—removing flowers after they have finished blooming—benefits your plants in more ways than one. The most obvious is that your garden will look neater without dead flowers drooping off bloom stems and spoiling your display.

Beyond that, deadheading can extend your flowering season, help keep your plants vigorous, and encourage an even better display of flowers the next year. Annuals will respond to deadheading by producing more flowers. You'll extend their bloom season by as much as several weeks. By removing spent flowers, your plants won't use up energy producing seeds. Instead, many shrubs, bulbs, and perennials will primarily direct their energy into leaf and root growth. The increased plant vigor will promote a better flower display the following year.

Preventing seed formation reduces weeding chores around plants that reseed readily, such as feverfew, foxgloves, and mulleins. Leave a few seed pods if you enjoy the self-sown seedlings or want to collect seed to sow next year. But keep in mind that deadheading will prevent fruit formation, a drawback on plants that produce attractive fruits, such as roses. Prolong the bloom season while still getting the showy fall fruit by stopping deadheading in the late summer.

Deadhead at least once a week. Collect your spent flowers in a bucket and place them in your compost pile. ❧

HAVE ON HAND:

▶ Pruning shears or garden scissors

▶ Bucket to collect trimmings

On clustered flowers, cut or pinch off individual blooms as they fade, or cut the whole stem at the base.

Trim off single-stemmed blooms just above uppermost leaves, or cut to the ground if stems are leafless.

Prune spent roses just above the uppermost five-leaflet leaf, or to a strong three-leaflet leaf.

On rhododendrons, pinch the base of the finished flower cluster and carefully snap it from the stem.

Staking

Annuals and perennials with long or slender stems often need help to stay straight and tall. Staking prevents tall plants from smothering smaller companions and keeps their flowers upright and visible.

The secret to successful staking is to support them before they need it. Once stems start to sprawl, it is very difficult to make them look natural again. Place supports in early to mid-spring so that your plants grow up through or around them, covering the stakes or wires.

Individual stakes are best for plants with a few tall stems, such as hollyhocks, delphiniums, and lilies. Choose a stake as tall as the plant's ultimate height. When you insert it firmly into the ground, it will be somewhat shorter than the stem and thus less visible. Tie plant to stake carefully, making a figure eight with green garden cord.

Large, bushy perennials, such as peonies, asters, and bleeding hearts, look better when supported by hoop-type stakes. You can buy them or make a similar structure with stakes and string.

Keep short, thin-stemmed plants from sprawling by "pea staking." Cut 9- to 18-inch lengths of twiggy branches (use your late-winter shrub prunings) and insert them firmly into the ground behind or within the developing clump. Snip off visible twig-stake tips if plants don't cover them when they mature.

At the end of the season, remove all of the stakes and wash, dry, and store until next season. 🌿

HAVE ON HAND:

▶ Stakes

▶ Soft string or yarn

▶ Scissors

1

SINGLE STEM. *In mid-spring, insert stake ⅓ of its length into soil, 3 to 6 inches from stem base.*

2

Tie a 6-inch string to stake, then loop it around the stem and tie it loosely. Repeat every 4 to 6 inches.

1

BUSHY STEMS. *Set four to six stakes evenly spaced around clump firmly into the soil.*

2

Tie string to one stake. Wrap free end around other stakes near top of all stems to form circle; tie again.

Watering

CHECKING MOISTURE. *Pull back mulch around plant to expose the soil, then dig a small, 6- to 10-inch-deep hole with a trowel.*

Proper watering is a large part of keeping your garden healthy and beautiful. When you choose the right equipment for the job and use it efficiently, you'll be able to irrigate with a minimum of time and water.

While many garden centers carry a dizzying array of watering equipment, your garden may require only a few basic items. A hose, nozzle, watering can, sprinkler, and soaker hose are among the most useful tools.

The rule of thumb is that a garden requires approximately 1 inch of water per week, either from rain or watering. In reality this can vary widely, depending on the plants you are growing, the amount of sun and wind, and your soil type. For instance, watering is less critical during cool, cloudy weather than in hot, sunny, or windy conditions. And sandy soil will need more frequent watering than soil high in clay. The best way to gauge the need for water is to check below the soil surface to see if the root zone is moist. (Perennials and shrubs generally form most of their roots in the top 6 to 18 inches of soil, while annuals tend to have more shallow roots.)

Water deeply rather than often. Frequent light sprinkling encourages roots to form close to the surface, where they will suffer quickly from drought. Moistening to a depth of 1 foot or so will encourage deep root systems that better withstand surface drying.

Water the soil and not the tops of plants. The easiest and most effective way to water an established planting is with soaker hoses. These hoses release water through holes all along their length. Water goes directly into the soil without wetting plant leaves, which can help avoid disease. Lay soaker hoses in the spring, before plants fill in. Cover them with mulch, leaving the connector end exposed. Attach to your water supply and let them run for two hours before checking soil. Turn water off when the root zone is moist.

HAVE ON HAND:

- ▶ Trowel
- ▶ Watering can
- ▶ Hose
- ▶ Sprinkler
- ▶ Soaker hose

HAND WATERING. *Use a watering can to irrigate container gardens and individual plants as needed; avoid wetting leaves.*

Look at and feel the soil on the sides of the hole. If the top 4 to 6 inches of soil are dry, it's time to water.

If top 4 to 6 inches of soil are moist, refill hole, test every 2 to 3 days until topsoil dries. Note time it takes soil to dry as rough gauge for future.

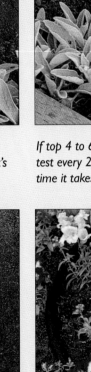

SPRINKLERS. *Seedbeds need frequent watering to keep them moist; water with overhead sprinklers until seedlings appear.*

SOAKER HOSE. *To water beds and borders efficiently and without wetting leaves, snake soaker hose through planting in spring.*

HERE'S HOW

SUPPLEMENTAL WATERING

During periods of drought, some plants will need extra irrigation to stay vigorous. You can give moisture-loving plants special treatment by sinking a small, unglazed clay pot into the soil next to the base of the stems. Place a cork in the hole at the bottom of the pot, and set the rim of the pot even with the soil surface. Fill the pot with water. The water will gradually seep out of the pot into the soil. Add more water as needed to keep the pot filled.

To supply extra water to new plantings, you can use a plastic milk jug instead. Poke one or two small holes in the base of the jug, set it next to the plant, and fill it with water. Refill as needed to replace the water as it seeps into the soil. Remove the jug once plants get established and start producing new growth.

Weeding

Weeding your garden doesn't have to be a major, ongoing chore if you take a little extra care before planting and employ several tricks to discourage weeds from taking over.

When you prepare a garden site, completely remove the grass or weeds already growing. Digging or tilling them into the soil won't eliminate weeds—it will simply spread them more evenly. It's especially important to remove the roots of creeping or deep-rooted weeds such as quack grass and dandelions. Roots will sprout new plants if left in the ground.

Keep in mind that weed seeds can live in the soil for many years. Each time you dig or till, a new crop of seeds is brought to the surface. One way to deal with them is a process called solarization. It will kill weed seeds near the surface, along with everything else in your topsoil. Should you use this method your soil will require heavy amendment with organic matter before you plant. If you'd rather not wait the 6 to 10 weeks solarization takes, try another trick. Prepare your site, then water thoroughly and wait 7 to 10 days. Hoe the weed seedlings that have sprouted, water again, and wait another 7 to 10 days. Hoe again, then plant. After using either method, disturb the soil as little as possible when you plant to avoid bringing up more weed seeds.

After planting, apply mulch to minimize further weed development. A layer of 2 to 3 inches will prevent light from reaching the soil and discourage weed seeds from sprouting. Weeds that do pop up will be easy to pull. Another method is to shade the soil with plants. Fill in around new perennial plantings with low-growing annuals for the first year or two, until perennials become established. Planting ground cover under shrubs and trees will provide a similar benefit and is an interesting change from mulch. 🌸

HAVE ON HAND:

▶ Spade or shovel

▶ Water

▶ Clear plastic (at least 2 mil thick)

▶ Hoe

▶ Hand fork or trowel

▶ Grass shears

SOLARIZING. *In early summer, prepare your site for planting by completely removing grass and weeds and by loosening the soil.*

PULLING. *Pull out weed seedlings by hand or with a hoe. This task will be easier when the soil is moist after rain or watering.*

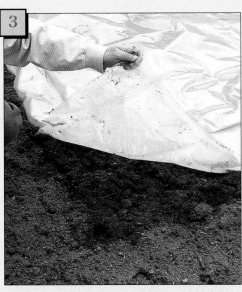

Water area thoroughly. Cover the soil with a sheet of clear plastic. Bury the edges of the plastic with garden soil to keep it in place.

Leave plastic covering in place 6 to 10 weeks; remove. Amend planting holes with organic matter. Don't disturb surrounding soil when planting.

DIGGING. *If weeds have several pairs of leaves, use a hand fork or trowel to dig out roots along with the tops.*

CUTTING. *If digging weeds will harm nearby plants, cut weeds to the ground every week or two until no new sprouts appear.*

HERE'S HOW

SMOTHERING WEEDS

If you don't have the time or energy to dig out an established patch of weeds, you can try smothering them. Cut weeds as short as possible with a mower or string trimmer. Cover the area with sheets of cardboard or a thick layer of newspapers, then top with a 4- to 8- inch layer of shredded bark or wood chips. Or cover the planting area with black plastic topped with 2 to 3 inches of mulch.

Leave the mulch in place for at least 1 year. During that time, add more mulch as needed to keep the layer at the right thickness. When you are ready to plant, rake off the mulch (and remove remaining paper, cardboard or plastic); then prepare the soil for planting as usual.

Fertilizing

To stay healthy and vigorous, your garden plants need both a steady and balanced supply of nutrients. Fortunately, it's easy to apply supplemental fertilizers to keep soil fertility at the right level for good plant growth.

Before adding fertilizers to your garden, take a soil test (see Testing Your Soil, page 10). You can then tailor your program to add only the nutrients that are lacking. Adding too much of a nutrient can be as much of a problem as not adding any at all.

In most cases, however, you'll be applying a "complete" or "balanced" fertilizer to your garden. It will contain nitrogen, phosphorus, and potassium—the three major nutrients that plants need for healthy growth. Nitrogen promotes lush, leafy growth. Phosphorus promotes flowering and fruiting, and potassium encourages a strong root system. The label of any fertilizer will have a series of three numbers—5-10-5, for example—indicating the available percentage of nitrogen, phosphorus, and potassium, respectively. To encourage flowering, the middle number should be higher than the other two.

The best time to apply organic fertilizers is when you prepare your soil for planting. Nutrients will be spread evenly through the root zone, where plants need them. You can add fertilizers after planting, but it will take longer for nutrients to reach plant roots. Dry organic fertilizers (manures, rock phosphate, granite dust) release nutrients slowly but steadily, so one application usually lasts several months. However, if your annuals, container plants, new plantings—or other flowers and shrubs—start blooming poorly or growing slowly during the summer, treat them to a dose of a liquid fertilizer such as fish emulsion or seaweed extract. Already in liquid form, it will immediately be available to developing roots. ❀

HAVE ON HAND:

▶ Balanced, dry organic fertilizer

▶ Shovel, spade, or tiller

▶ Hand fork

▶ Liquid organic fertilizer

▶ Watering can

▶ Sprayer

APPLYING DRY FERTILIZERS. *Scatter a balanced organic fertilizer over the soil before planting; dig or till into top 6 inches of soil.*

APPLYING LIQUID FERTILIZERS. *Immediately after planting, water with diluted fish emulsion or seaweed extract.*

Feed perennials and bulbs in the fall or spring. Spread fertilizer or compost over the soil; scratch it in lightly with a hand fork.

Fertilize shrubs in the fall or spring. Pull back mulch, scatter fertilizer or compost over the soil, then replace mulch.

Give annuals and container plants a mid-season boost by watering them with liquid fertilizer during the summer.

Spray perennial and shrub leaves with liquid fertilizer in early to midsummer; apply in morning or on a cloudy day to prevent possible leaf burn.

HERE'S HOW

MAKING COMPOST TEA

Compost makes a good dry fertilizer, either worked into the soil before planting or scattered around growing plants. Your plants can also enjoy the goodness of compost in liquid form if you treat them to a cup of compost tea. It's easy to make:

Use an old pillowcase or a piece of burlap 2 feet square to hold a shovelful of finished compost. Tie the top of the bag with string, then drop the bag into a 5-gallon bucket of water.

Let steep for 7 to 10 days; then lift out the bag. Apply the wet compost to your garden or return it to the compost pile. Add water to dilute the remaining liquid to the color of weak tea. Use as you would fish emulsion or seaweed extract, to water new plantings or to feed annuals, perennials, and shrubs.

Mulching

A mulch is any material that is used to cover the soil around and between plants. Using mulch effectively can help make your garden a long-term success. Although mulches can be inorganic (nonliving) materials, such as black plastic or gravel, organic mulches—those derived from formerly living materials—are preferable because they provide extra benefits in the garden.

Both organic and inorganic mulches will shade soil, preventing weed seeds from sprouting and minimizing water loss due to evaporation. Mulch will also keep soil from splashing up on plants, keeping flowers clean and reducing the likelihood of disease. In winter, mulches moderate soil temperature changes, which prevent freeze-and-thaw damage (see Winter Protection, page 130). In addition, an organic mulch, such as chopped leaves, shredded bark, or other material, provides an attractive background for flowers and foliage. Organic mulches also improve your garden soil as they break down over time and release nutrients and organic matter.

When you select a mulch, consider appearance, availability, and price. Coarse mulches, such as wood chips, are well suited to shrubs and trees; fine-textured mulches, such as shredded bark, are more attractive in flower gardens and other high-visibility areas. Don't overlook the mulch materials found right in your yard: grass clippings and shredded leaves are two. To cut down on expense, buy mulch for beds near the house and use home-made mulches for less visible areas.

While mulches can do wonders for your garden, they can also cause problems if not handled properly. Mulches are ideal hiding places for slugs, snails, and other soil-dwelling pests. If you have serious damage to your plants (leaves or flowers that have large holes or have been totally eaten), rake off the mulch and allow the soil surface to dry out before replacing it. If damage continues, reduce mulch by half or stop using it. Mulch can also hold moisture against leaves and stems, which can encourage rot to develop. Keep all mulches at least 2 inches away from the base of stems. ❦

HAVE ON HAND:

▶ Hoe
▶ Shovel or pitchfork
▶ Mulch
▶ Trowel

APPLYING ORGANIC MULCH. *Cultivate the area thoroughly to remove existing weeds before applying mulch.*

MANAGING MULCH. *During the growing season, pull or dig out any weeds that surface through the mulch.*

Use a shovel or pitchfork to spread mulch evenly over the cultivated soil. A 2-inch layer of
mulch is usually sufficient for most plantings.

Pull mulch away from the base of each plant
with your fingers, so the mulch is at least
2 inches away from plant stems.

Check the depth of the mulch layer 2 or 3 times
a year; add more mulch if needed to maintain
enough thickness to foil weeds.

In early spring, rake mulch from beds to let the
soil warm up and dry out; replace the mulch
layer in late spring.

HERE'S HOW

SPECIALTY MULCHES

While materials such as shredded bark, chopped leaves, and wood chips are traditional favorites for mulching, you may also be able to find other excellent mulches, depending on the nature of your local industries. Some industry by-products can work just as well as more common mulches and are usually available at reasonable prices.

In some areas gardeners can buy bags of cocoa shell mulch from candy or chocolate factories. Cocoa shells make an attractive, lightweight, easy-to-apply mulch; they also have a pleasant chocolate aroma for the first week.

If you live near a mushroom production area, you can usually find mushroom compost (the "soil" that's left after the mushrooms are harvested). Look for mushroom compost that has been aged for a few months; fresh compost can be high in salts or other materials that can damage your plants.

Other specialty mulches include grape pomace (pulp), apple pomace, buckwheat hulls, pecan shells, and seaweed, to name a few. To find out which materials are available in your area, talk to gardening friends in your community or check the garden-related classified ads in your local newspaper.

Trellising and Training

Directing plant growth with trellising and training can keep plants in top form. The techniques described here don't take much time, but they can work wonders by turning floppy or spindly plants into attractive, well-formed ones.

Trellising is the technique of choice for plants that have long, trailing stems, such as wisteria vines. A well-constructed trellis will support your vines' top growth while providing an attractive background for leaves and flowers. When selecting a trellis, consider the vine you'll be growing on it. Twining vines (such as Lonicera honeysuckles) can grow on just about any trellis. Vines that climb with tendrils (such as crimson glory vine) or twining leaf stems (such as clematis) grow best on a trellis with thin crosspieces—½-inch wide or less. You can grow them on a

thicker trellis, but the vine would then have to be tied as climbing roses are.

You can train your plant by taking steps to direct its growth and flowering. Proper pruning and staking (see Staking, page 117) are essential but there are other important techniques as well. If you pinch off the top bud, for example, lower buds will be encouraged to grow. This is a great way to promote dense, bushy growth—and more flowers—on many leafy-stemmed plants such as clematis (also see Deadheading, page 116). Pinching can help delay flowering, so you will have flowers over a longer period of time than you normally would. Stop pinching in early July so that flower buds have time to form flowers for the fall. Pinching is also a promoter of sturdy stems, which can help reduce your staking chores.

Disbudding is another training method. By cutting or rubbing off sideshoots, the plant is encouraged to put its energy into the top flower bud. Each stem will then produce only one flower, but that bloom will be large and showy. Disbudding is not often used on vines but is common with bedding plants such as chrysanthemums and dahlias, and even hybrid tea roses. ❧

HAVE ON HAND:

▶ String or soft twine

▶ Scissors

▶ Grass or pruning shears

ATTACHING A VINE TO A TRELLIS.
Cut a piece of string or soft twine 6 inches long. Tie it around a crosspiece on your trellis.

PINCHING. *Use your thumb and forefinger to pinch or snap off individual shoot tips, just above a leaf or pair of leaves.*

Gently pull the loose ends around a stem; tie again, leaving some slack around the stem. Trim extra string so it won't be visible.

Tie again every 6 to 12 inches. Check every few months to make sure ties are not cutting into stems; use a looser tie if needed.

SHEARING. *If plant has too many stems to pinch, cut top growth back by ½ of total length of stems with grass clippers or pruning shears.*

DISBUDDING. *Pinch or rub off sideshoots; leaving top flower bud. Don't remove leaves that grow directly from the stem.*

HERE'S HOW

ATTACHING TRELLISES TO WALLS

When you install a trellis next to a wall, use small blocks of wood as spacers to hold the trellis 2 to 3 inches away from the structure. This will allow air to circulate between the vine and the wall, discouraging disease problems and minimizing damage to the wall as well.

To make future wall maintenance easier, attach the bottom of the trellis to hinges, and use hooks and eyes to hold the top of the trellis to the spacers. When you must reach the wall, simply unhook the top of the trellis. Carefully lower it away from the structure and prop it on a ladder. When you are finished with the wall, raise the trellis again and rehook.

Fall Cleanup

When fall frost nips at your flowers and leafy growth slows down, it can be tempting to give up on your garden. However, it's worth taking the time to do a final cleanup before winter sets in. Putting your garden to bed properly can prevent problems next year, and gives it a tidier appearance for the winter months.

Dead leaves, flowers, and stems provide ideal overwintering sites for insects and disease organisms. You can remove these problems before they develop. If you know a plant is diseased, discard its top growth in your trash or bury it in an out-of-the-way spot. Otherwise, it's safe to add plant debris to your compost pile.

HAVE ON HAND:

▶ Pruning shears

▶ Leaf rake

▶ Water

▶ Rags

▶ Spading fork

▶ Hand fork

Cut back spent flower stems after bloom to prevent plants from dropping seed and self-sowing. While a few self-sown seedlings may be welcome, some plants can produce copious amounts. (Foxgloves, columbines, and coneflowers are a few examples.) If you like, leave just one or two flower heads to get a few seedlings without creating a problem.

While it may seem like a good idea to let fallen leaves accumulate on beds, it's best to rake them off regularly. It's also a good idea to rake mulches away from shrubs and perennials in mid-fall. Mulches and fallen leaves provide ideal shelter for mice, voles, and other animal pests, encouraging them to nest in your garden. They'll feed on your plants through the winter, chewing roots or devouring crowns and buds. By removing these sheltering materials, pests will make their homes elsewhere, minimizing the risk to your plants. It's safe to replace the mulches once the ground is frozen.

Some perennials, such as purple coneflowers, sedums, and asters, have attractive seed clusters that appeal to wintering birds. Many ornamental grasses also provide winter interest. If you enjoy the look of these plants, wait until late winter to cut them down. ❦

Pull out dead annuals, roots and all. Cut back dead growth on perennials. Start a new compost pile with these materials.

Dig dahlias, gladiolus, and other tender bulbs before frost or when leaves turn brown. Dry and store indoors for the winter.

Fall is a great time to get many garden jobs done. The air is cool but the soil is still warm, providing ideal conditions for root development. When you plant, transplant, or divide plants at this time of year, they'll settle in well and be in prime condition for growing next spring. Here are a few other gardening jobs that you can do in the fall:

Take soil tests and add any needed amendments.

Dig new garden beds for planting in fall or spring.

Fertilize perennials, bulbs, and shrubs with compost.

Sow perennial seeds; plant bulbs.

Drain and store hoses.

Clean, sharpen, and store garden tools.

Fall is also the time to review the past year's triumphs and tragedies. In your gardening notebook, make a note of disease or pest problems you encountered during the year so you'll be able to take the correct control measures early next year. Also, jot down new ideas and plant combinations you want to try so you'll be ready when the spring shopping season arrives.

Rake mulches and fallen leaves away from shrubs and perennial beds. Shred leaves for mulch or add to compost pile.

Dump annual container plantings into the compost pile. Rinse clinging soil out of containers; dry and store indoors for winter.

Do a final, thorough weeding to catch weeds you missed earlier, as well as to eliminate newly sprouting cool-weather weeds.

Remove stakes from the garden. Discard twiggy stakes. Wash soil off permanent stakes and let them dry before storing for the winter.

Winter Protection

For cold-climate gardeners, winter is a time to dream, to think back on successes of the season past and plan for next year's plantings. But while you are comfortable indoors with your catalogs and coffee, your plants are coping with winter's stresses: fluctuating temperatures, drying winds, and hungry animals. Protecting your perennials and shrubs to help them weather the winter will be time well spent.

If your perennials and bulbs are naturally adapted to your climate, they will tolerate the winter cold on their own. Top growth dies back to the ground, and roots are insulated by the soil. Problems arise when warm spells are followed by cold snaps, especially in late winter. Warmth tricks plants into producing new growth, then frost kills the tender shoots. But you can use a trick as well. Cover soil with winter mulch to keep it evenly cool. (Wait until soil is frozen, to avoid providing shelter for pests.) Choose a loose, lightweight mulch: shredded leaves, pine needles, or straw. (Do not use hay, and remove all mulches in early spring.) Snow, if you're lucky enough to have it, is excellent, insulating the soil from swings in air temperature.

Shrubs need different protection. Top growth is subjected to dry winter wind, which draws moisture out of stems that frozen roots can't replace. To minimize winter damage, stop fertilizing shrubs by midsummer; this stops the tender growth that is most susceptible to drying. Water thoroughly before the ground freezes, and place burlap screens on the windward side of the plant to block wind. Foliage can be protected by antitranspirants (available at garden centers).

Protect the bark and stems on shrubs from rabbits and other small critters with wire-mesh "collars." To foil deer, however, you'll need to put an 8-foot fence around your yard or create temporary fences 6 feet tall around individual plants. ✺

HAVE ON HAND:

▶ Water

▶ Pruning shears

▶ Mulch

▶ Evergreen boughs

▶ Antitranspirant

▶ Burlap and stakes

PROTECTING PERENNIALS. *If the fall has been dry, water regularly until top growth dies back; then cut back dead tops.*

PROTECTING SHRUBS. *Water deeply around shrubs before the ground freezes to ensure that the root zone is moist.*

Once the soil is frozen, add a 3- to 6-inch layer of mulch over the bed. Any falling snow will be a bonus, increasing the insulation.

When the soil has frozen, replace the mulch you raked off in the fall; add more, if needed, to keep the layer 2 to 3 inches thick.

Where winter snow cover is unreliable or nonexistent, lay evergreen boughs over mulched plants to provide extra protection.

Spray evergreen foliage with an antitranspirant according to package directions, or install a burlap screen to block wind.

HERE'S HOW

HANDLING FROST HEAVES

Frost heaving is the result of fluctuating temperatures around unmulched plants. Alternating freezing and thawing pushes plant crowns out of the soil, breaking the roots and exposing buds and tender roots to drying winds.

Mulching frozen soil in late fall or early winter and covering beds with snow, as described, will usually prevent this problem. But it's a good idea to walk through your garden during warm spells to spot any plants that may have been heaved out of the soil. If you can, push the tops back into the soil; otherwise, pile on extra soil or compost to cover exposed roots. Replant heaved clumps at their proper level once the soil thaws in spring.

A Guide to Winter Protection

COLD PROTECTION

Many plants adapt to cold weather if they've been exposed gradually. Keep dormant plants evenly cool so that rapid thawing and refreezing won't damage them.

STRAW
A loose, lightweight winter mulch for perennials and roses. Apply a 4- to 8-inch layer evenly over the bed after the soil is frozen. Carries fewer weed seeds than hay.

PINE BOUGHS
Evergreen branches provide excellent insulation for perennial beds and small shrubs. Wait until the soil has frozen to lay over plants.

WIND PROTECTION

Winter winds dry buds and evergreen leaves. To prevent browned leaves and dead shoot tips, water soil thoroughly in fall and use barriers to block the wind.

FABRIC SCREENS
Attach burlap or landscape fabric (sold in garden centers) to stakes driven into the ground. Make the screen a few inches taller than the protected plant.

LATH FRAMES
Set up a lath screen (such as snow fencing) around individual plants; attach it to stakes. The laths can be horizontal or vertical, as needed.

PEST PROTECTION

When other food is scarce, garden plants are prone to damage from deer, rabbits, mice, voles, and other animal pests. Such damage is hard to fix, so is best prevented.

MULCH MANAGEMENT
Rake mulches 1-2 feet away from the base of plants in early to mid-fall. This will encourage mice and voles to make their homes elsewhere.

BURLAP WRAP
One effective, although not especially attractive, way to discourage deer damage is to cover whole plants with burlap. Tie with string or twine.

Winterizing Garden Accessories

Plants aren't the only things in your garden that need protection from rough winter weather: furniture, bird baths, and other items need some help, too. Protect your investment by spending a few minutes preparing your garden accessories for the cold. 🌿

1

Inspect fences, trellises, arbors, and benches for damage; make repairs. Wash tables, chairs, and other lawn and patio furniture. Store portable pieces indoors, or stack securely in a spot out of the way and out of the wind.

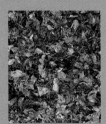
CHOPPED LEAVES
A lightweight, readily available winter mulch for shrubs and perennials. Apply a 4- to 6-inch layer over beds once the soil has frozen.

INDOOR STORAGE
To minimize cold damage to potted perennials and shrubs, move them to a cool, protected place such as an enclosed porch or garage.

SINKING POTS
Another option for protecting potted plants is to sink pots other than those of terra cotta or concrete into the ground. A vegetable garden or annual bed is an ideal location to use this method.

FENCES
Slatted fences provide good wind protection. Avoid solid fences; turbulence caused by wind flowing over the top can actually lead to more plant damage.

WINDBREAKS
Plant deciduous or, better still, evergreen hedges or evergreen trees on the windy side of your garden in order to block damaging gusts.

ANTITRANSPIRANTS
Commercially available antitranspirant sprays coat leaves with a waxy barrier that prevents them from drying out. Apply according to package directions.

CHICKEN WIRE CAGES
This is another way to discourage browsing deer. Make cage at least 6 feet high; attach to stakes driven partially into the ground.

WIRE COLLARS
Shield stems from mice and rabbits with a 1- to 2-foot collar of ¼ inch wire mesh. Sink the bottom 2-3 inches deep into the soil so pests can't burrow.

REPELLENT SPRAYS
Repellents aren't infallible but may prevent minor damage. Apply commercial repellent sprays according to package directions.

2

Clean bird feeders thoroughly with water and a stiff brush to remove dirt and old seed; allow them to dry completely before filling and rehanging. Scrub bird baths. Bring ceramic and metal bird baths indoors for winter; keep plastic and concrete outside.

3

In water gardens, cut or pull dead leaves and stems off hardy submerged plants and plants growing at perimeter. Bring cold-tender plants indoors. Remove submersible pumps; clean thoroughly and store in a dry place for winter.

Troubleshooting

PROBLEM	CAUSE	WHAT TO DO
Seedlings suddenly topple over and die. Any seedling is susceptible, but annual phlox and sweet alyssum are especially prone.	Damping-off, a disease caused by a fungus that forms in the soil and attacks seeds and the roots of young seedlings at ground level. Cold, wet conditions encourage the fungus.	Before sowing seeds indoors, drench planting flats with approved fungicide. Use a sterile, soilless planting medium. Do not overwater. Provide good air circulation. Plant in well-drained soil.
Leaves develop dark brown spots or lesions, foliage yellows, plant dies. Affects annuals such as calendula, chrysanthemum, geranium, heliotrope, lobelia, zinnia; perennials such as aster, chrysanthemum, delphinium, foxglove, iris, and phlox.	Leaf spot disease, caused by a number of fungi or bacteria and spread by insects, contaminated tools or even splashing water. The organisms thrive in moisture.	Remove and destroy all infected leaves. Thin plants to increase air circulation. Water overhead only in the morning. A fungicide will protect healthy plants, but will not cure infected ones.
Upper leaf surfaces have pale spots; undersides of leaves are covered with orange, brown or reddish powdery spots. Leaves may wilt; plant growth may be stunted. Affects many annuals such as baby's-breath, chrysanthemum, hollyhock, lobelia, morning glory and snapdragon; perennials such as bee balm, columbine, liatris, and lupine.	Rust, a disease caused by a fungus that thrives when days are hot and humid and nights are cool.	Remove and destroy infected plants. Water early in the day so plants can dry before nightfall. Spray with sulfur or approved garden fungicide. In fall, discard infected leaves and stems. Some varieties of snapdragon and chrysanthemum are rust-resistant.
Leaves, stems, flower buds are coated with fine, white powder. Plant and flower shape may be distorted. Prevalent late summer and fall. Susceptible annual plants include phlox, bellflower, fuchsia, spider flower, sweet pea, verbena, and zinnia. Susceptible perennials include aster, bee balm, delphinium, and phlox.	Powdery mildew, a disease caused by a fungus. The fungus is spread by wind and water, and it thrives in both hot, dry weather and periods of high humidity.	Grow susceptible plants in full sun with good air circulation. Remove and destroy infected plant parts. Water overhead only in early morning. Sulfur-based fungicides prevent the disease and eliminate it on infected plants, anti-desiccants are also effective. Mildew-resistant varieties of bee balm and zinnia are available.
Tips, leaves, centers of flowers blacken, buds may not open (peonies). Often accompanied by a fuzzy, gray growth. The problem occurs most often in cool, damp conditions. Annuals affected include forget-me-not, fuchsia, geranium, heliotrope, lobelia, petunia, snapdragon, stock, and sunflower. Perennials include the peony.	Botrytis blight, also called gray mold, a disease caused by various fungi.	Avoid overhead watering and provide good air circulation. Cut away any infected areas of plants and destroy them. Use fungicide to control the disease. Cut infected stalks to the ground in fall and destroy. As perennial growth starts in spring, spray with a systemic fungicide to prevent recurrence.

PROBLEM	CAUSE	WHAT TO DO
Leaves curl, wither, may turn yellow or have a sooty appearance. Flowers may be distorted in shape. Plant may be stunted. A shiny substance appears along stems and leaves.	Aphids (plant lice), ⅛-inch-long cream, green, red, black, or brown semitransparent insects found in colonies on buds, leaves, and stems. They secrete a sticky, shiny substance that attracts ants.	Wash plants with a spray of water and diluted soap solution. Ladybugs, beetles that eat aphids, may be introduced into the garden.
Oblong or irregular-shaped holes appear in leaves and flowers. Eventually, plants may be stripped of all foliage. Many annuals, including balsam, China aster, flowering tobacco, phlox, and zinnia, are susceptible. Many perennials are affected as well.	Any of several beetles, including Colorado potato, cucumber, and Japanese, ¼- to ½-inch insects with hard shells.	Small colonies of beetles can be handpicked and destroyed. Japanese beetles can be caught in baited traps. Beetle larvae can be destroyed with milky spore, a bacterium that is fatal to beetles but harmless to both plants and animals.
Leaf surfaces show areas with light green or brown tunnels that later turn black. Leaves may lose color, dry up, and die. Affects many annuals such as chrysanthemum, dahlia, morning glory, nasturtium, and verbena. Can affect perennials such as columbine, chrysanthemum, delphinium, and primrose.	Leaf miners, flies that lay their eggs on leaves. When the eggs hatch, the microscopic pale green larvae tunnel into the leaves.	Control is difficult. Pick off and destroy infested leaves as they appear. In the fall, cut infested plants to the ground and discard them. Since organic waste attracts flies, keep your garden well weeded.
Leaves become speckled yellow or reddish, surface becomes dull. Foliage may curl and wither. Black specks are visible on the undersides of foliage. Eventually, webs appear on plants. Particularly evident in hot, dry weather. Many annuals are affected, as well as perennials such as columbine, daylily, delphinium, iris, phlox, Shasta daisy, foxglove, hollyhock, candytuft, and chrysanthemum.	Mites, pinhead-sized, insect-like creatures. Spider mites suck the juice from leaves.	Keep plants well watered; spray the undersides of leaves with water or a diluted soap solution regularly. Ladybugs are natural predators.
Entire plants become discolored. Shaking a plant will cause a white cloud of specks to appear. Growth may be stunted. Especially affects annuals calendula and coleus; perennials such as hibiscus, columbine, lupine, primrose, and chrysanthemum.	Whitefly, a white, 1/16-inch insect that collects in colonies on the undersides of young leaves.	Check for signs of whitefly before buying bedding plants. Whiteflies may be controlled with insecticidal soap or an organic spray. They are attracted to the color yellow. Try placing yellow flypaper in your garden to help control whitefly population.

Glossary

ACID (acidic) a soil with a pH lower than 7.0; also known as a sour soil; opposite of alkaline.

ALKALINE a soil with a pH higher than 7.0; also known as a sweet soil; opposite of acid.

ANNUAL a plant that sprouts from seed, grows, flowers, sets seed, and dies within one growing season.

BARE-ROOT the condition of having no soil around a plant's roots.

BIENNIAL a plant that produces only leafy growth during the first growing season, then flowers, sets seed, and dies after living through one winter or a certain period of cool temperatures.

BULB specifically, a compact structure composed of a central growth bud surrounded by food-storing leaves; also used as a general term to include true bulbs, corms, rhizomes, tubers, and tuberous roots.

BULBIL a small, bulb-like structure that forms along a plant stem, at the joint of a leaf and the stem.

BULBLET a small bulb that develops underground, from the base of a mature bulb or from the stem produced by a mature bulb.

CANE stem; often used in relation to roses.

CLIMBER a plant that produces long stems that climb up a support or another plant.

COMPOST an organic material composed of decaying plant and animal materials.

CORM a bulb-like structure composed of a swollen stem surrounded by a papery tunic (covering).

CROWN the point where the roots join the aboveground parts of a plant.

CULTIVAR a group of plants that have been chosen and propagated for a particular characteristic, such as flower color or height, and are genetically uniform. Cultivar names are always given in single quotes (as in 'Moonbeam' coreopsis).

CUTTING a piece of stem, leaf, or root that has been removed from a plant and exposed to certain conditions to produce new roots and shoots.

DEADHEADING removing dead flowers.

DECIDUOUS a plant that drops its leaves in fall and produces new foliage in spring.

DIEBACK death of shoot tips and leaves due to disease or damage. Also, a leafless dormant period before regrowth in regular cycle.

DIVISION the technique of separating a plant clump into several smaller parts.

DORMANT (dormancy) a plant in a "resting" state, usually during a period of low or high temperatures. Plants often die down to the roots when they enter dormancy only to resprout when suitable growing conditions return.

DOUBLE DIGGING the process of loosening the top 12 to 16 inches of soil by removing the top layer of soil with a spade or shovel, loosening the lower layer with a spading fork, and replacing the top layer.

DOUBLE FLOWER a flower with more than the normal number of petals found in that species, usually in more than one row.

EVERGREEN plants that hold their foliage for more than one growing season.

FLAT a shallow tray used to hold soil or pots.

FORCING providing the right combination of temperatures to encourage growth and flowering; usually used in relation to growing bulbs for indoor flowering in late winter.

FUNGICIDE a compound applied to plants or soil to kill fungi.

GRAFT UNION a swollen area near the base of a stem, where the top of one plant has been joined to the roots of another; often seen on roses and some shrubs and trees.

GROWING SEASON the time between the last spring frost and the first fall frost.

HALF-HARDY used to describe a plant that may be damaged by cold temperatures in a particular area. Half-hardy annuals usually need to be started indoors and set out after the last spring frost; they can generally tolerate more cold once they are established. Half-hardy perennials may survive mild winters outdoors but usually need to be brought indoors or protected with mulch to survive cold temperatures.

HARDENING OFF the process of gradually exposing plants started indoors to outdoor conditions.

HARDPAN a dense, compacted layer below the soil surface.

HARDY used to describe a plant that lives and thrives in a given area. Often related to cold tolerance, hardiness can also be affected by heat, rainfall, and other conditions.

HEAVY SOIL soil with a high clay content.

HUMUS decayed organic matter.

HYBRID the offspring produced from genetically different parent plants. Hybrid plants often are more vigorous and productive than either parent.

INSECTICIDE a compound used to kill insects.

LAYERING the process of treating a shoot so it will form roots while still attached to the parent plant.

LEACHING the loss of nutrients from the top layer of soil due to water draining down through the soil.

LIGHT SOIL soil with a high sand content.

LIME a calcium compound. Calcitic lime contains mostly calcium carbonate; dolomitic lime contains calcium carbonate and magnesium carbonate. Ground limestone (also called agricultural or garden lime) is best for garden use; quicklime and hydrated lime are more caustic and can damage plants.

MULCH a material applied over the soil surface to keep the soil moist, moderate soil temperatures, or suppress weeds.

NATURALIZE to set out plants in masses to create a natural-looking effect; often used in relation to bulbs planted in grassy or woodland areas.

NODE the point where a bud or leaf (or a pair of leaves) joins a stem.

NURSERY BED a special plot set aside for growing young plants and bulbs until they are large enough to survive in the regular garden.

ORGANIC a general term applied to mulches and other materials derived from decomposed plant or animal products; also used to describe the process of growing plants without the use of synthetic chemicals.

PATHOGENS disease-causing microorganisms.

PERENNIAL a plant that can live for more than two years.

PERLITE white granules of a volcanic mineral that has been exposed to high heat; often added to potting soil to improve drainage.

PESTICIDE a compound used to kill insects or mites.

pH a measure of a soil's acidity or alkalinity on a scale of 1.0 to 14.0, with 7.0 being neutral. A pH below 7.0 is considered acidic; above 7.0 is alkaline.

PINCHING using your thumb and forefinger to remove a shoot tip, generally to encourage a plant to produce bushier growth.

RHIZOME a thick, horizontal, underground stem.

ROOTBALL the mass of roots and potting soil visible when you remove a plant from its pot.

ROOTSTOCK the root system of a grafted plant.

RUNNER a horizontal, aboveground stem that produces roots at the nodes.

SELF-SOWING (self-seeding) a plant that drops seeds, which grow into seedlings.

SHOOT a branch, stem, or twig.

SHRUB a bushy, woody-stemmed plant, usually with multiple stems at ground level.

SINGLE FLOWER a flower with a single row of petals, usually four to six.

STANDARD plant trained to grow as a single, leafless stem topped with a bushy "head."

TENDER plant susceptible to frost damage.

THINNING removing individual stems or whole plants to give remaining stems or plants room to develop without crowding.

TOP-DRESSING adding compost or fertilizer to the soil surface around plants.

TUBER fleshy underground stems with "eyes" that develop into roots or leaves and flowers.

TUBEROUS ROOTS swollen, fleshy roots joined by a bud-bearing crown.

VARIETY a naturally occurring variant of a plant; indicated by the word "var." in a plant's name (as in *Imperata cylindrica* var. *rubra*).

VERMICULITE a lightweight, flaky material produced by exposing mica to high heat; often added to potting mix to improve water retention and drainage.

WOUND a cut or damaged area on a plant.

Index